Single·Voices

Single·Voices

The Chemist by Roy Clarke

Royal Enclosure by Sheila Hancock

Sandy Comes Home by Barry Humphries

The Last Supper by Carla Lane

Ginger by Bob Larbey

Some Enchanted Evening by John Sessions

BBC Books

All photographs © BBC

Published by BBC Books,
a division of BBC Enterprises Limited,
Woodlands, 80 Wood Lane, London W12 0TT

First Published 1990

The Chemist © Roy Clarke 1990
Royal Enclosure © Sheila Hancock 1990
Sandy Comes Home © Barry Humphries 1990
The Last Supper © Carla Lane 1990
Ginger © Bob Larbey 1990
Some Enchanted Evening © John Sessions 1990

ISBN 0 563 20898 8

The song on page 38 is
© Dick James Music Ltd,
c/o Polygram Music Publishing Ltd,
Chancellors House,
Chancellors Road,
London W6 9QB
Words and music by Chris Arnold, David Martin and Geoff Morrow

The song on page 43 is
© EMI Music Ltd,
30 Gloucester Place,
London W1A 1ES

All rights whatsoever in these plays
are strictly reserved and application
for permission to perform, etc, must be
made in advance, before rehearsals
begin, to the appropriate artist's agent

Set in Linotron Plantin by
Goodfellow & Egan Ltd, Cambridge
Printed and Bound in Great Britain by Mackays of Chatham Plc
Cover printed by Richard Clay Ltd, Norwich

Contents

Acknowledgements

To all those within and without the BBC who made the series possible, and to Clive Mendus for playing the hand in *The Chemist* and Suzie Gee and Luke Anthony for playing the Greek couple in *Sandy Comes Home*.

Introduction

The monologue has long been used as a dramatic device through which a character expresses emotions and tells a story, from ancient Greek drama through to music-hall entertainers and comedians (Arthur Askey, Stanley Holloway and Joyce Grenfell for example), and to the most recent successes of Samuel Beckett, Harold Pinter, Dario Fo, Alan Bennett and Willy Russell. There is something strangely seductive about one person exposing their private personal life to us as an audience, and we are often called upon to use our imagination and concentration to their fullest extent. And are we always wise to accept their stories at face value? In *Single Voices*, for instance, is Sheila Hancock's Doreen as well-in with royalty as she imagines? And is Carla Lane's butcher, who buttonholes us to listen to his tale of infidelity, such a mistreated husband after all?

When work began on this six-part series of monologues, I especially wanted to concentrate on writers and performers from the world of light entertainment, some of whom had not worked a great deal in drama before. It was very exciting to bring together such diverse and original talents as Roy Clarke, David Jason, Sheila Hancock, Barry Humphries, Carla Lane, Michael Angelis, George Cole, Bob Larbey and John Sessions. All of them contributed their own inimitable styles, and created characters and situations which are not always comic, often bringing poignancy to the fore. The worlds of light entertainment and drama do not often come together (writers and performers can easily be categorised) so it was refreshing and stimulating to be brought into close contact.

David Jason's roles in *Only Fools and Horses*, *A Bit of a Do*, *Porterhouse Blue* (for which he won a BAFTA award) and Roy Clarke's *Open All Hours* have entertained many and earned him great respect. In 1988 he won the TRIC BBCTV Personality Award. In his performances he always manages to combine a rare mix of comedy and pathos. It was splendid to be able to bring David and Roy Clarke together again for *The Chemist*. Roy's other credits include, *The Last of the Summer Wine*, *The First of the Summer Wine*, *Potter* and *Rosie*, but he has written for drama as well, including the series *Flickers* and *Pictures*. *The Chemist* is a quirky piece in which we are introduced to Vernon Duxley, a man in the middle of a marital crisis. How can or should he respond to his dilemma? He speaks to the video camera in his shop about his appalling weekend, using the screen in a way not seen in the other monologues.

Sheila Hancock's career has managed successfully to embrace light entertainment and drama. Not only has she been in *The Rag Trade* and *The Bedsit Girl* on television but she has acted and directed for the Royal Shakespeare Company and the National Theatre, and gained an OBE. Most recently her performances in *Jumping the Queue* and *Prin* have attracted deserved recognition. This is the first play she has written for television and she creates Doreen, a cheery soul, who lives for her love of famous personalities and royalty. There are many Doreens in the world, both young and old, and this is a tribute to their loyalty and perpetual tragic optimism.

Barry Humphries' extraordinary creations of Dame Edna Everage and Sir Les Patterson are well known. He has many fans. In 1988 he was named Showbusiness Personality of the Year. Sandy Stone is a more poignant, lyrical character, a Melbourne ghost who finds it hard to adjust to changed times in suburbia, where the old have become redundant, often consigned to little flats by their daughters-in-law, or worse still, sent to homes for the 'bewildered'. This monologue was first performed as part of Barry's stage show, and the character has been with him since 1959, though portraying Sandy as a ghost is a new development. Although there are the familiar shafts of black humour in Sandy, there is a poetic feel to him which marks him out from Barry's other more outrageous personae.

Carla Lane started writing for light entertainment with a hundred episodes of *The Liver Birds* (in which Michael Angelis featured as Lucian, the brother with the rabbits). Since then, of course, there has been *Butterflies*, *As I Walked Out One Morning*, *The Mistress*, *Solo*, *Bread*, and an OBE. There has always been a strand of serious drama in Carla's work, but it has been some time before she could be persuaded to concentrate on it. Her witty monologue *The Last Supper* is about a butcher, played by Michael Angelis, who laments his divorce from a vegetarian. This cleverly structured piece is written like a detective story, with clues interspersed throughout and the twist left right to the end.

My admiration for George Cole began in the days of Flash Harry and St Trinians, and now of course, his Arthur Daley is a television immortal. It was good to reunite George with Bob Larbey who worked together on the West-End hit *A Month of Sundays*. Bob's career in light entertainment speaks for itself, he has collaborated with John Esmonde on *The Good Life*, *Ever Decreasing Circles*, *Please Sir* and *Brush Strokes* amongst many, as well as writing the very popular *A Fine Romance*. His subtle black humour and precise observation evoke the grotesque world of the over-60's club which Ginger chooses to incite to rebellion with disastrous results. Ginger, the jaunty, unglamorous Lothario, who lusts hopelessly after Miss Probert is an indomitable personality.

John Sessions has been affectionately nicknamed 'Renaissance Man' because he is a man of so many parts. His appearance on *Whose Line is it Anyway?*, *On the Spot* and *Napoleon* have made him famous for his razor-sharp quickfire characterisations. However, he has taken on serious roles as well, in amongst others, *Porterhouse Blue* and *The Common Pursuit*. In his monologue *Some Enchanted Evening* (which is the first drama he has written for television), he creates Bobby Buffet, an astringent though mediocre American musical director, who brings a show to London and lives a lonely existence in a hotel with no piano. When he finally gets the piano he demands, he finds it has an emotional string attached, and tragedy ensues.

All six dramas are characterised by those who have written and performed them, and so have different styles and different emphases. It is good to see those involved doing something 'different', creating characters and situations which they have not touched on before, and creating as a whole a varied and idiosyncratic collection of monologues.

Fiona Finlay.

The Chemist

A love story

ROY CLARKE

VERNON DUXLEY David Jason

Produced by Fiona Finlay
Directed by Robert Knights
Designed by Gary Pritchard
Music by Bill Connor

We are looking at a small-town chemist's dispensary somewhere in Yorkshire in the rather dim early-morning light, which percolates through a glazed and barred window. The place is empty. It contains the usual shelves laden with boxes of pills and other chemist's sundries. There is a table, a computer, a sink, and a hatch to the shop. We hear the shop door being unlocked and opened, and through the hatch we can see the lights in the shop switched on. We can hear the chemist's voice.

Eddie! I've brought in my video. I'm setting it up here. Bit of time and motion study. I don't want to be disturbed.

The dispensary door opens, the dispensary light is switched on. The chemist is moustached. But the moustache is neat, the suit is neat. He almost certainly has dainty feet. He is carrying the video camera. He looks at the battery-driven clock on the wall and checks it against his watch. He puts the camera down on the table while he removes his jacket. He hangs it on the hook, from which he takes his white laboratory coat, and he puts this on. There is something slightly odd about his walk. His white coat on, he turns his attention to the camera. He picks it up from the table and looks around the dispensary for a suitable place to park it. He selects a place on one of the shelves and puts the camera into position.

The screen grows light somewhat unprofessionally, and we get the first glimpse of our chemist through his video camera. He is far too close to the camera while he adjusts its controls. He steps back a pace to a more comfortable position where we can see him, head and shoulders, and he addresses the camera.

Monday morning. Day One of the reconciliation with my wife. I am to be master in my own house.

He lowers his voice for this and turns and closes the hatch. Again he checks the wall-clock against his watch.

It's been a traumatic weekend. During the crisis we seldom spoke in less than a shout. My mother would have been appalled. I was raised not to shout. Had she fallen into water my mother, I swear, would have drowned making only the most delicate noises. Her little finger would have gone down gracefully three times. My wife, by contrast, girds herself with drama. Extracts from the passing moment its maximum turmoil. Enjoyed this weekend the meatiest role of her career. I have to talk to someone. Of things too intimate for friends. This needs a stranger. And you're the perfect stranger.

The chemist is fidgeting a little and finding something shy-making about his first attempt at camera. He has another look at the clock, then he issues a command through the hatchway into the shop.

It's time, Eddie. Raise the blinds. Open the doors.

He switches on the computer then he turns back towards the camera.

Never late in fifteen years. It's that kind of proud record which adds up to much that my wife despises about me.

He busies himself about the dispensary, making ready for the morning's trade, continuing to address the camera as he does so.

Fifteen years. That's how long I've had my own business. It's a small shop. It's a small town. Mine the only pharmacy. Nobody dies round here without some interference from me. Dies naturally that is. Our two murders of recent years I picked up no business from. Accidents are snapped up by the state. A good percentage of suicides however do remain loyal to their local pharmacist.

On a couple of occasions we have seen the chemist look rather longingly towards the telephone. It's as if he would love to make a call, but is hesitating.

My name is Duxley. D.U.X.L.E.Y. Vernon Duxley. Not the sportiest of names, I don't know why the hell mother chose it unless it whispered well.

A hand appears in the hatch and sticks a prescription form onto a spike. The chemist turns away from the camera for a moment, picks up the prescription, reads it and walks to his bench, and begins to fill it. He talks to the camera as he works.

Repeat prescription for Mrs Rodway. A formerly fashionable lady with a tendency to wear a hat.

He counts a few pills into a small container.

Mrs Rodway requires 75 milligrams daily of a certain substance just to see her through the week. The removal, surgically or otherwise, of Mr Rodway would almost certainly improve the clinical picture.

The chemist selects a label and begins writing briefly on it. He sticks the label onto the container. The chemist puts the completed prescription onto the hatch. He turns away back to the camera. Behind him a hand appears and removes the pills. He closes the hatch. He looks once again at the telephone. He half reaches towards it, then changes his mind. Another prescription appears in the hatchway. The chemist takes it and reads it, and closes the hatch and walks to his bench.

My wife's name is Marlene, which you might say should have told me something, but you can't hold people accountable for their names – I have a Vernon to vouch for that. The deficiency is her mother's. Marlene! Those two syllables encapsulate her mother for all eternity. A Marlene breeder if ever there was one.

The chemist reaches out and rubs his finger along the computer keyboard, he grimaces with distaste at the feel of dust. He walks towards the hatch and calls through.

Eddie, let's have a good dusting out there this morning. Get the girl to go through the shelves. Take everything down, wipe all the bottles.

He turns away from the hatch and walks back to his bench. The chemist writes another label and sticks it on his bottle. He takes the bottle to the hatchway. He returns to the camera with another look at the phone.

Marlene was a first for me in several departments, not least of which was physical. She had me in a state of almost terminal randiness, untypical for me. I'd had my brushes with lechery, but in a very amateur capacity. Some student fumbling, a relationship or two. Once on campus in a sexual act I realised that I was memorising the side effects of chloramphetamine. There was an exam approaching but it wasn't as if it was going to get there first. Until I met Marlene my own sexual proclivities remained fairly moderate on the Beaufort scale. I was already settled here in my own business, still living with mother. I played a little golf. I filled a non-performing role with the local operatic society and a similar with a rather shaky soprano. Looking back it's plain my life ran a tepid course. I was not unhappy. Then along came Marlene.

He glares at the phone as if he hates it.

Tedium is seriously underrated.

He reaches for the telephone, lifts the receiver and dials a number. It begins to ring at the other end and he waits for an answer. It continues to ring. His expression fluctuates from impatience through anxiety to irritation.

She should still be in bed unless she's going out. I'll kill her if she's gone out. She promised me she wouldn't see him again. I was really firm about that. Of course she could be going out without seeing him again. Let's be fair.

He puts down the phone.

Also she could be in the bathroom. She got me to buy her the town's most expensive bathroom. It's her Dallas fantasy. That's where she'll be – in the bathroom.

The hands bring two more prescriptions. The chemist takes them absently. He reads them equally absently, or so it seems as he walks back to his bench to begin preparing them.

How long can she be in the bathroom? She'd better not be long in the bathroom. If she's long in the bathroom it means she's grooming herself for whoredom and she's up to something.

He stops his work on the prescriptions and returns to the phone. He picks it up angrily and dials again. The number begins ringing. He stands there listening to it ring, growing angrier and angrier. He slams down the phone.

She's up to something. I know the formula. Excessive time in the bathroom equals adultery.

He returns to work on the prescriptions. He works for a while with a quiet intensity. He performs his duties and writes his labels automatically almost, with much on his mind. We can feel the anger.

I'll kill her. I'll lock her in the house. It's a bungalow. I'll lock her in the garage. I'll teach her to love me and only me or I'll – lower the limit on her credit cards.

He completes the prescriptions and puts them in the hatchway. He turns back towards the camera.

We had a terrible weekend. Things were said.

He goes to his jacket pocket and takes out a slim paperback.

Cruel things. I wear a knee bandage. Not all the time. Just periods when my knee is playing me up. It's an old sporting injury. I twisted it in a morris dance. Another thing she finds hilarious. Morris dancing was good for my shorter leg, but in the face of her derision I put away my bells. One makes these gestures for a marriage. But I reserve the right to keep the knee bandage. You may have noticed some slight irregularity in my walk. I don't really think of it as a limp – more of a lisp. My leg has a not unattractive lisp.

He fills an electric kettle. He splashes himself and the paperback in the process.

Damn!

He puts the kettle on, then wipes his coat and the book.

Since this weekend I see clearly now that she regards me as deficient in the macho department. The woman is unreceptive to the neater graces. Apparently she finds something irresistibly comic in my knee bandage. It seems it's not so much a bandage as an orgasm inhibitor. A process at which, so she tells me, I am already uncannily deft.

He limps about the available space seeking to burn off his anger.

Right!

He taps the paperback.

'Isometric Exercises for the Busy Executive'. I bought it before we were married. Then I met Marlene and the last thing I seemed to be short of was exercise. However. If she wants macho she can have macho. See how she likes it when I begin to brutalise her.

Opening the book on the bench he begins trying an exercise. This consists of pushing with the palm of one hand against a firm surface. We watch him growing redder.

Ingenious stuff this. None of your muscular drama. Just scientific, small movements of a precision nature.

He stops for breath then begins working the other hand. After a minute of intense strain which shows in his face he stops again.

Do it anywhere. Good to record these first faltering efforts. Then, when I'm honed down to pure steel, I'll be able to look back and smile.

The kettle is boiling. He makes a drink.

I met my wife here in the shop. It was almost winter, but she was tanned and freshly back from some concrete sun spot. I was in the shop. She came in off the street, undid her blouse, and asked me for something for her insect bite. I remember gaping – me who could never stand heights – down this dizzying cleavage. It was exactly the place I would have bitten her. Nearly did. I brought her here into the dispensary and prepared a lotion. I was gone even then. She had overwhelmed me with that bitten breast. And with every button further as I applied a soothing lotion I was lost. She wore some frivolous and gossamer half bra, and it was clean. I had been raised to respect the clean. Clean I believed was character. Before I had finished ministrations down that valley of delights I loved her.

The chemist paces somewhat agitatedly backwards and forwards in front of the camera.

I wanted this woman, like none other, and she was going to walk out of my life. I had dabbed her breast with camomile and that was going to be the extent of our relationship. 'What do I owe you?' she said. I have no facility for those opening moves in the game of sex. Not like some I know. There's one at the golf club. He goes through women like streptococcus. Practically an epidemic. The swine can do a lovely chip shot too. Gregory Stiles. Old 'Call-me-Greg'. The contents of his jockstrap formidably bigger than his IQ. But he owns a pub and discothèque, and would have known how to stop this woman walking out of my life.

He spends a minute doing another exercise.

'What do I owe you?' she said. 'To be my guest at dinner,' I said, naming the most expensive local restaurant. And she agreed. I'd done it. Pulled off an assignation with this marvellous slightly nibbled female just recovering from a divorce. God how I dressed for that first date. With what care I mixed and matched the raciest items from my wardrobe. I'd never looked lovelier. I called at her house. Her mother greeted me at the door. 'What's wrong with your leg?' she said.

He sips his drink. Behind him another prescription comes into the hatch. He takes it and goes to his bench and works on it.

Her mother preferred me in my white coat. As did Marlene. I was nearly as good as a doctor. We honeymooned in Venice.

He sips his drink.

I got dysentery. In my absence my wife became over-familiar, I thought, with a waiter. On the last day I felt better. We walked by moonlight in St Mark's Square. My wife smelled of garlic.

Lost in his thoughts he stares rather sadly into space. A noise in the shop brings him back. He takes the completed prescription to the hatchway. He walks to the telephone and dials his number again. He listens to it ringing. He puts down the phone.

There are numerous reasons why she might be out. Since she married me Marlene has become a woman of wide and varied interests.

Another prescription comes in. He takes it and goes to the bench.

Initially it must be admitted I found my new wife to have a somewhat limited capacity to respond to my intellectual passions. The range of her concerns at that time could perhaps best be summed up as Italian waiters. It was clear to me that I would have to begin educating my bride. In return I would make every effort to accommodate her. I grew a moustache, I had my hair styled, I began to dress a mite more aggressively. I bought an open sports car.

He returns to the hatch with the completed prescription. He turns back to the camera.

She likes the sports car.

He takes down the telephone directory and begins looking up a number.

She's probably out in it now. As for my clothes, she confessed she likes me best in a white coat. She wasn't joking. It got so if I wanted to make love to her I had to wear the damn thing. God knows what roles I play in her fantasy hospital series. Do you know what she bought me for our anniversary. A stethoscope. She won't make love without it. Our foreplay was becoming almost entirely diagnostic.

He picks up the phone and dials the number.

Hello, this is Mr Duxley. Is my wife there this morning? Her appointment's tomorrow is it? I see. Thank you.

He puts down the phone. He returns the directory to its place. He half sits on the table and looks at the camera.

Not at the hairdresser's. Could be anywhere. As I say, she's now a woman of wide and varied interests. She owes me that. I began by reading to her in bed. At first she made boredom noises but gradually it began to fascinate her. In time she became so hungry for this education she'd never had, that when she saw me on love nights reaching for my white coat, she'd say, 'Not tonight, Vernie, why don't you read to me?' During our second winter she signed on for night classes. I never thought she'd last, but before long she was doing Alienation in the Modern Novel, and on Thursday nights Hidden Repressiveness in Bourgeois Culture. I discovered later that she was screwing the tutors. She cottoned on very quickly to the pleasures that can be had from adult education. When I pointed out to her, I thought not unreasonably, that her adulteries ought not to be subsidised by the rates, she became indignant and accused me of being a typical example of the repressiveness of bourgeois culture.

He takes down the telephone book and looks up another number. He picks up the telephone and dials another number. He listens to it ring. It's answered.

Is that the Squash Club? Hello, it's Mr Duxley here. Is my wife playing there this morning? She isn't. She's not booked in for later? I see. Thank you. I must have confused the days.

He puts down the telephone. He turns a page of the book and begins another exercise. This one involving strengthening his neck. Another prescription comes in. He takes it and goes to his work-bench.

I welcomed her next foray into self-improvement at first. It seemed safer. She fell in with the feminist movement whose scouts are active in Further Education. I applauded her new seriousness even if it meant that on the increasingly infrequent occasions that we made love she had to be on top. As she became more involved with the sisters she told me tales that set my hair on end. I began to get the picture about sexual harassment. The sisters are experts.

He resumes his neck exercises, in the course of which he gives himself a slight crick.

It didn't last. Try as she might, Marlene wasn't made that way. She stopped reading the *Guardian* and went back to the softer attentions of men. I say men deliberately. It would have been nice if she'd come back to me, but the truth is she came back to the male gender collectively.

As he tests his neck, gently, we can see, also quite clearly, the pain occasioned by his wife. He puts the completed prescription in the hatchway. He turns back to the camera.

Thing I learned about love is – it can feed on anything. Even infidelity.

He spends half a minute trying to remove the crick from his neck. Abandoning the neck he tries another arm exercise but occasionally it twinges his neck.

I adjusted. And if she'd shown an ounce of discretion I could have gone on adjusting. She had it made. Damn it I'm still doing the cooking. But no, she has her mother's flair for bad taste. My wife gives me the ultimate . . .

He makes a rude finger gesture at the camera.

She falls in love. I find this obscene. Her sexual romps I could cope with, as little more than an extension of aerobics. Which is how, I'm sure, she regarded it. The next move after squash. But I'd come home to find she'd been crying. This woman not only humiliates me, but is now growing so dark about the eyes she looks like a panda. She loses her appetite. I'm still doing the cooking, and now the bitch won't even eat it. When she goes out to see *him* she wears dark glasses. *He's* not supposed to see what a mess she looks. I'm in love with a panda.

He does more exercises – favouring his neck.

I can't bear to see her so unhappy. I begin to feel anger towards this stranger who is wasting my wife.

More exercises, this time hurting his neck. He paces, rubbing his neck.

One of the foundations, however, of our accommodation together is that I don't ask questions. But she was in breach of the rules anyway. You live with these situations by pretending that they don't exist. And there she was sniffing at tea-table, pacing the room at nights. She was making it impossible for me not to see. 'Is he married?' I asked her. Yes he was married. Did I know the man? Yes I knew him. She began to weep. She looked at me with those big panda eyes.

He lies on the bench for a further exercise.

We had the kind of long, ruthless, no holds barred, cuts to the bone kind of row we hadn't had for months. I think we both enjoyed it. It was almost like old times.

He gets off the bench.

I finally got through to her that I wanted to help. If I knew the man perhaps I could make some suggestions how she could handle him better. This she thought was disgusting – my offering to help her make progress with another man. 'You don't love me,' she said. 'All right,' I said, 'forget it. Eat your ravioli.' But she was zooming through stratospheres of emotion far removed from ravioli. And then finally she told me his name. Screamed it at me in defiance. Then I couldn't eat *my* ravioli. Greg Stiles. Good old Call-me-Greg. Of all the pricks in the universe she has to fall for Call-me-Greg.

He throws himself into another exercise. We watch him working the anger off.

This is a muffin with funny stickers in his car rear window. With a tattooed forearm. With aftershave in stereo. With a gift for being there when things fall off lorries. With a snout at home with the piggiest pleasures and this is humping my wife, and what's more without sufficient enthusiasm to make the process acceptable to her.

Behind him another prescription comes into the hatchway. He snatches it up in a flaring temper and looks at it.

Who wrote this? How am I supposed to read these damn things?

He takes the prescription over to his bench, complaining as he goes.

The medical profession! Five years' university to learn to scribble.

He begins putting together the prescription. He pauses halfway through. His shoulders slump. He turns to the camera.

Why do women go for such dickheads? Explain that away you sisters. Can't they see? Don't they know one when they find one? I mean how can you miss the basic lack of nobility of old Call-me-Greg, at fifty yards in the dark? It's not as if he hides it. He wears bright red trousers for golf. He has a musical keyring. He strips at stag nights. He keeps his sexual score card printed on his jockey shorts. The tally of his victories round that cockpit. Enemy knickers going down in flames.

The chemist goes back to completing the prescription.

If you made a list of everything the women's movement claim to hate about men, Call-me-Greg's just about got the lot. So how come I see this twot going through women with the same casual ease as he plays a round of golf. On the fairway or at fornication I seldom see the bastard slice. There's something basically insecure about the foundations of the women's movement. Deep down under all that self-righteousness a terrible knowledge is working. That if they poke so much as a nose outside their own sex they're going to fall for some prawn like Call-me-Greg.

Still in a bad mood the chemist slams the completed prescription on the hatchway ledge.

They've got this gene somewhere that selects for dickheads.

The chemist picks up the telephone book again.

Well that's it for me. End of the line.

He thumbs through the book.

The wrath of a Vernon Duxley can be terrible. I warned her. No more Call-me-Greg.

He finds the number and picks up the telephone. He dials the number and changes his voice.

Mister Greg Stiles please. My name? – er – Wilberforce. What's it about? I'll tell you what it's about. It's about a – a waterbed. That's it. A waterbed. He asked me to call him with reference to a waterbed. Did he leave a number where he could be reached? If you wouldn't mind. Yes please.

The chemist picks up a pen and waits to record the number.

3 0 5 1 4 2, thank you.

The chemist puts down the phone. He glares at the camera.

Yes he left a number where he can be reached.

He paces in extreme agitation.

My home number.

The chemist lifts up the phone again and dials his own number, his face contorted with anger.

Three oh five one four two. And as for you lady.

But when the phone is answered he makes the effort and puts on a calmer voice as if he's suspecting nothing.

Hello love, it's me. Just ringing to see how things are. You seemed pretty upset when I left this morning. In fact you sound a bit breathless now. I see, just out of the shower. I see, well long as you're OK. Just thought I'd ring. Tell you how glad I am we patched things up. No. Don't let me detain you. You go back to whatever it is you were doing. Yes. I love you too.

The chemist puts down the phone. He paces the room in a quiet but very real agitation. He has forgotten the camera. When he turns there are tears. He remembers the camera. He sniffs and quickly wipes his eyes. He sighs and turns to look at the camera.

There they are. In my house. In my bed. After all the promises.

The chemist walks towards his shelves and begins selecting from the array of bottles and pills.

Though they despise me as a man a little prudence would have kept some respect for the pharmacist.

He takes down a container of pills.

For you my faithless love.

He puts the container on his bench and continues looking through the containers on his shelves for another bottle. He selects one and reads its label.

And what we have here is a comprehensive solution to the Call-me-Greg epidemic.

The chemist studies the two pill containers. He looks at his hand and is proud to find it not shaking.

How calm it is once you've made the decision. There's a moral here somewhere. Malice is good for you. Sod Isometrics.

He sends the book flying.

It's going to take a little while. Before the symptoms appear. But I can be patient. Terrible is the patience of a Vernon Duxley.

He lifts up the two containers to the light and smiles in a sinister manner at them.

It will be a pleasure – watching for the first signs.

He smiles and nods at the bottles in turn.

This will take the rhythm out of your strokes. By these gifts, Marlene is going to grow hair on her chest, chin and faithless upper lip, and Call-me-Greg is about to become locally famous for his high-pitched voice and outstanding knockers.

Chuckling with glee the chemist puts the two containers into the pocket of his jacket on the hook. He turns away still chuckling then stops and the smile disappears. He limps back to his jacket and retrieves the two phials. He checks which is which.

I can't grow hair on that unblemished chest. I love that chest.

He returns Marlene's phial to the shelves. He glares at the other phial.

But him!

He takes Greg's phial back to his jacket. He pauses.

She loves.

He studies the phial and we know he's looking at Greg. We see anger, perplexity, hate and finally resignation. He puts that phial too back on the shelf. He glares at the camera.

I'll fight fair or not at all. He'll hurt her. He'll hurt her. She's going to need somebody to come back to – somebody without a knee bandage.

He picks up his book of exercises. An idea, a resolve occurs to him. He rolls up his trouser and removes his knee bandage. He tosses it into a bin. We leave him bravely doing his exercises.

Fade out.

Royal Enclosure

SHEILA HANCOCK

DOREEN Sheila Hancock

Produced by Fiona Finlay
Directed by Michael Jackley
Designed by Gary Pritchard
Music by Bill Connor

*We are in front of the railings of a basement flat in Hammersmith. The camera
takes us through the railings to a heavily netted window. Through the window to
a bird-cage. Inside is a rather mangy budgerigar. His cage is full of toys,
including a mirror. Through the cage to the face of a middle-aged woman. This is
Doreen.*

Hello my little cock sparrow. Is Mummy late then? I am very sorry sir she
said. But you just wait till you hear . . . Oh hold on. Let me get my puff
back. I'll put this down, then I'll tell you my wonderful news.

*We see she has two large carrier bags from John Lewis. We look round her
bedsit. Neat, clean, but full of bric-à-brac. Curtained kitchen area. Old-
fashioned gas fire with meter. A photograph of the Royal Family over the
fireplace and various pictures of Barry Manilow and Danny Kaye around the
room. An ancient Singer treadle sewing machine. An old-fashioned radiogram.*

(*To budgerigar.*) Look at this lot then. Cost me a fortune, even if they didn't
knowingly undersold me. But you get what you pay for and I wanted the
best for this. The best ever. Look. A nice bit of shantung. How about the
colour? Eau de nil it's called. Refined en't it? And here's the pattern. Nice
and tasteful. Vogue – none of your Butterwicks for this outfit. (*To camera.*)
No fear. This is going to be the most important day of my life. A
momentuous occasion. It might change the course of history. (*Daunted.*) Oh
dear.

She takes off her hat and coat.

Oh. I'm all of a tizwoz. Must pull myself together. I've got a lot to do before
he comes next month. (*Bird chirps.*) Don't worry Face-ache. No one will
ever take your place. Not even him. Much as I love him. Give us a kiss,
come on. Strewth, it's freezing in here. (*Lights gas fire.*) Warm my posterior,
if you'll excuse the expression.

She stands with her back to the fire, lifting her skirt slightly.

Oh that's lovely. Oh dear, this place is a tip. I'll have to get it shipshape and
Bristol fashion before he comes. Take the curtains to the launderette or
something. It will be a bit of a come-down after what he's been used to. I'd
better get rid of Barry and Danny. (*To Budgerigar.*) Not you, silly. Mr Kaye

and Mr Manilow. Don't want him getting jealous. I'm prepared to give them up for him because he needs me so desperately. Pilloried. That's what he is, pilloried. Let's have a cuppa.

She goes to the kitchen area and makes the tea.

Oh, that reminds me. I must get my Mum's cups out and give them a rinse. Ever since her wedding she was saving them for a special occasion, bless her. I'm sorry to say she passed on before she'd had one. But I know she would want me to get them out now. 'Let's have a bit of la-de-da,' she'd say. I shouldn't think he'd be jealous of Danny now he's passed on. I'd hate to take his picture down. He was my first love after all. He was gorgeous was Danny. I mean he was dead funny, but he could be really serious too. Sitting on the edge of the stage at The Palladium talking about life. I couldn't help loving him. It was the dog that clinched it though. I had made him this felt toy. It was very pretty, although I say so as shouldn't. It had a flower in its mouth. I left it at the stage door. Then during the show that night – I went every night he was on – wonders will never cease, he suddenly produced it and showed it to the audience. I could have died. He asked who had sent it – who Doreen was – but I was struck dumb. I went round to the stage door afterwards but it was packed with ignorant people shouting and screaming. I tried to get to him but they elbowed me out of the way. My Mum, bless her, brought me up to believe that little girls should be seen and not heard so I wasn't going to lower myself. I wasn't going to behave like an animal. An animal with elbows. It's not in my nature. So I never got to him to tell him I was Doreen. But it didn't matter really. I was glad the dog made him happy. His life wasn't easy. He wasn't blessed with a happy union. Not like my Mum and Dad. War hero my Dad was. Wonderful man. A saint. To be honest, I don't remember him too well myself. I was only six when he went away to war. But my Mum was always telling me how wonderful he was.

Picks up photograph of man in army uniform.

Don't he look handsome in his uniform? It's strange, I can only remember how it felt. On the back of me legs. I think it was the last time I saw him. Embarkation Leave they called it. We had Sunday tea. I'd bought a pint of winkles and shrimps from the barrow on the corner – miserable old sod the man was – and there was Mum's Victoria sandwich. She made it with dried egg but it still rose, she was a miracle. I was in my spotted organdie – you always wore your best on Sundays in those days – and fresh white ankle socks and patent shoes cleaned in milk. I looked the bees knees. I sat on his lap singing a song with him and I could feel his uniform all scratchy on my bare legs.

   She sings.

> There'll be bluebirds over
> The white cliffs of Dover
> Tomorrow just you wait and see.
> There'll be love and laughter
> And peace ever after
> Tomorrow when the world is free.

His breath smelt of tobacco. And I shouldn't wonder if he hadn't had a little beer. I remember that. And my Mum's face when the telegram came. I remember that too. It was only a few days after that a land-mine went off down the road and we first saw the Royals. The dear old Queen Mum – or Queen as she was then – came with the King. Funny thing – I don't remember much about my Dad but I can see them two clambering over the ruins as if it was yesterday. My Mum got right up close to the King. She said they were so real. She said it made up for everything. They didn't actually speak to my Mum. But they did to Mrs Fricker whose house had gone. She said they said how sorry they were. Wasn't that wonderful? My Mum said if she could have talked to them she'd have said 'Thank you for coming' – and she would too. She was like that my Mum. She didn't care. But she just did her curtsy and gave them a wave.

   Which reminds me – rabbiting on here. Where's my Royalty magazine?

   She goes to a pile of magazines.

It was in last month's. Here we are. Right. Let's have a go. Put one foot behind the other. Lock your knees. What's that mean? Oh er. (*She follows the diagram.*) Is that it? Now bend. I can't. That can't be right. Oh I see. That's better. Oh dear, gives me gyp in my housemaid's. Still, a bit of practice each day and it'll ease up. Oh look at you Danny. You think I've gone dulally tap? I haven't told you have I? My wonderful news. Prince Philip is coming to the Baths. Tara. Can you believe it? That policeman must have told him I worked in the ticket office there and now he's coming.

They say it is to present some prizes for the Adventure Programme, but we know better don't we?

To camera.

Well of course it all fell into place the minute Mr Beringer told the staff. July 23rd 1988. The day our eyes met. He was giving a speech at the Annual Banquet of the Worshipful Company of Fruiterers – don't know what about – fruit I suppose. Anyway, he was running in like he always does in his monkey suit, when suddenly he stopped – like this – turned and looked – like this.

Mimes a look of curiosity followed by raised eyebrows and a weak smile and nod.

Well, my legs were spaghetti. I don't know how I got home on them. The next night at the Dinner for the Badgers' Preservation Society – he's the President and Honorary Life Fellow of that (he never stops, love him) – well I was outside as usual when it happened. This copper came up to me, plainclothes he was, but they have that look don't they? And he said, 'We've noticed you are always at His Royal Highness's functions. Why is that?' I knew then that I wasn't mistaken. I knew then that Philip felt the same way about me as I did about him.

It was tippling down, which was just as well 'cos he thought it was rain dripping off the end of my nose. I never cried when my dear Dad died or Bert left, or even when my Mum passed on, but I did then. I was so happy. Oh I'm off again. Silly cow.

Pull yourself together Doreen for heaven's sake. There's a lot to do before he comes here. Shut up you daft hap'orth and make a list.

She does so between chuckles and sniffs.

Go to black.

Come up on Doreen's bedsit. Day. Doreen is on her hands and knees. There is a sheet on the floor. The paper pattern is pinned to the material which is now cut out and she is marking tucks, etc., with tailor's chalk. She has a mouthful of pins. She is working all the way through the scene, eventually getting to the sewing machine.

These darts are going to be very naughty. But they should give a nice bust-line. Now this skirt. I've cut it wider in the back 'cos of me curtsy. I want to go really low. (*She practises*.) Getting better.

I wonder if that copper is in on it, the one who asked me where I work. 'May I have your name and address and place of work please madam.' He was very polite, he took down all my particulars. I was very cagey when he asked me why I was always at Philip's do's in case he was in the dark. 'Me and my Mum have been to all the royal occasions since I was a little girl,' I said. 'We slept in The Mall more times than you've had hot dinners,' I said. 'Oh,' he said, 'is that so?' 'Yes it is so,' I said. 'We take our thermos and sleeping bags the night before, come rain or shine, so we can be in the front row behind the barriers,' I said. 'Well I never,' he said. 'Yes,' I said. 'We danced outside Buck House on V.E. night before you was born, young man,' I said. 'And we was there on Coronation Day, Charles and Di's wedding, you name it we've been there,' I said. 'And since my Mum passed away I've kept the flag flying on my own,' I said. 'Well, how would they manage without you?' he said. 'Exactly,' I said. I think he was being a bit sarky. I told him, I said, 'I could have been evacuated to America in the war like Thelma Jones up the road', but the little princesses were staying, so my Mum said 'What's good enough for Elizabeth and Margaret Rose is good enough for you.'

I might have been Elizabeth Taylor now. But I'm glad I'm not because I wouldn't be getting ready to go off with a real prince would I? Which is more than she's done, for all her jewels and her violet eyes.

Doreen stands up.

Gawd's strewth, I'm not as young as I was. But then neither is he. He needs a bit of peace and quiet. They were at him again today. About his grouse shooting. Well why shouldn't he? They're his grouse and they sound miserable bloomin' birds anyway. He needs to get away from it all sometimes. I mean look at him now. Zooming off in Concorde. Working his you-know-what off in Barbados. Then straight back and before he knows it – Hanlow Baths. It's too much for anyone. I'll see he takes it easy. I won't mind if he wants to have a little shoot. Mind you, there aren't many grouse round Hammersmith I shouldn't think. But I'll see he has a good time.

One thing I want to do is take him to the Waldorf Tea Dance. It's lovely there. All the ladies in their nice frocks and the men spick and span. It's just like the olden days. Everyone polite and nice. No ignorance. I always sit up behind the balustrade and watch, but when I take Philip we'll have a dance down on the floor. And all eyes will be upon us.

She dances ecstatically, singing in an old-fashioned but true voice.

Can't smile without you
Can't smile without you
Can't laugh and I can't sing
I'm finding it hard to do anything.
You see I feel glad when you're glad
Feel sad when you're sad
If you only knew what I'm going through
I just can't smile without you.
You came along
Just like a song
And brightened my day.
Who'd have believed
That you were part of a dream
Now it all seems
Light years away.
Can't smile without you.
Can't smile without you.

With constant key changes 'à la Manilow' she is now in a very high treble.

Oh blimey. I started too high. Oh it will be like a fairy-tale. It will make up for all the times I've watched Barry sing that song to other women. Even when I bought a seat in the front row I never managed to get up on stage in time. All the animals with elbows got there first. I'll have to still write to him because I don't want to let him down. And I get such nice letters back.

She takes out an ornate wedding-type album.

This last one. I wrote after that article in the paper being rude about his nose. Well I got this lovely letter back. It doesn't mention the nose business but it told me all about what he was doing and when he was coming to England next and says how lovely his new record is. See.

She shows a computer-type fan letter reply.

Isn't it wonderful he can find time to write to me when he is so busy?

No I don't want to lose touch with Barry. I couldn't have managed without him when I was married to that horrible creature. My mother warned me but I wouldn't be told. He seemed polite enough before we were married. But after – well the less said the better. Suffice it to say if it hadn't been for Barry I couldn't have borne it. Reeling in here – Oh well, least said soonest mended. He knew he couldn't compete with my Barry. So he skedaddled off the night of Barry's Blenheim Palace concert.

When I came back he'd gone. 'Good riddance,' I thought. Then I lit what was left of my candle from the concert – we all held them at the end, it was beautiful – and I sung a quick chorus of *It's a Miracle* and wiped Bert out of my mind for ever. My Mum was delighted. She said I'd have another man here over her dead body, which unfortunately it will be. But I should think she would make an exception with Philip because she was as fond of him as I am.

She always preferred refined people. Like Danny my first love. He was elegant and sophisticated. A gentleman from his toes up. It was his long legs that attracted me. If you'll pardon me saying so. He had such lovely trousers always. The way he acted the fool it was a wonder they stayed looking so neat and tidy, but however much he wiggled they always fell nicely. Must have been a very good cloth I should think. I mean in *Minnie the Moocher* he darted all over the place.

She sings some Danny Kaye gobbledegook with actions. Loud music from upstairs somewhere.

Here we go. No peace for the wicked. Wherever you go that infernal row. You can't walk along the street without yobs going by with horrible great wirelesses blaring out. You sit on the bus and they have got things clamped over their earholes going tsk-tsk-tsk . . .

Music subsides.

Blimey another miracle. I was only fourteen when I first saw Danny but I knew my own mind even then. None of the local louts compared with him. Uncouth. So I didn't bother with them. I remember that's what caused the rift with Auntie Edna. She asked me if I had got a boy and I told her I was waiting for one like Danny Kaye or my Dad. And she said she didn't know about Danny but randy drunks were ten a penny. Well my Mum nearly

killed her. Quite right too. It was a wicked thing to say. My Dad was loyal
to my Mum till the day he died – she used to tell me that over and over. My
Mum was a stickler for loyalty and so am I. I mean I feel badly about
coming between Philip and the Queen. We don't want another upset like
the Windsors do we? But I have to follow the dictates of my heart and if he
needs me I am putty in his hands.

Ooh, I must do my nails nice. I'll put that on the list. Let's have a look,
what have I got left to do before the big day?

Give myself a perm. New petticoat and knickers. Speak to the Landlord
about the condition of the toilet. Practise curtsy.

She curtsies and the music from upstairs returns.

And tell him to do something about that bloomin' noise.

She puts on a record of marching music.

This'll drown them out!

Go to black.

*Come up inside the ticket office of Hanlow Baths. It is a small room with one
door and a grille window through which the tickets are sold. The room is full of
game machines, boxes, tables and chairs. Doreen is in her new finery, complete
with beflowered hat on her new perm. A sort of downmarket Queen's outfit. There
is a lot of bustle going on outside the window.*

What a carry on. At this rate I shall have a heart-attack before he gets here.
I am all of a tremble. It's that young 'erbert Ronnie's fault. I always keep
my office nice and clean. Right pig's dinner they've made of it. Not even a
by your leave neither. He starts bunging all this rubbish in. ''Ere, what you
up to?' I said. 'What?' he said like he does. 'What's all this?' I said. 'What
you going on about?' he said, all snotty like. 'Putting all this rubbish in my
office that's what I'm going on about, young fellow-me-lad.' I said, 'I'm not
having this,' I said. 'Mr Beringer's orders,' he said. 'Oh,' I said. 'Oh.'
Anyway Philip won't come in here. Well, what can you do? He came in
through the Town Hall entrance, saw all that lot, and now he's in the pool.
Well not actually in the pool.

She looks through the window.

It looks nice out there now they've painted it. Mind you I don't know how long it will last because it was all a bit of a kick, bollock and scramble. Just slapped the paint on over all the peeled bits and the dirt. I should think that it'll flake off by next week again. Still, as long as it's nice for the Prince. What's the time? Oh, not long to go.

She looks out.

I've got a lovely view from here. I quite understand about not being in the line. Well of course, as Mr Beringer said, he's got to let the professional people stand there. I mean there's the Arts and Recreation man and the Parks and Open Spaces, and lots of local nobs. And the man that gave the paint. There's only room for one of the staff and of course that has to be the manager that goes without saying. Anyway the rest of them have got to be on cockroach watch. They've got to stamp on any making their way towards the entourage. Us and the regulars are used to them, but they're hardly the thing for a Prince are they? And I'm going to be in my window. Mr Beringer's going to do his best to make sure a gap is left in the line so I can see the Prince. And he me. Little does he know what will happen then. Mind you, neither do I. Oh dear.

They have chosen some nicely behaved children to be in the pool as well as the prize-winners so it won't be the usual bedlam. Oh, I would hate Philip to see it on a normal day. I never come out of my office no more. I only looked at the pools once, that was enough. All that flesh thrashing about and screaming and hollering, echoing round the tiles. I don't like it. I could swim free if I wanted but I'm not exposing myself. You don't see the Queen in a swimming costume do you?

What's the time? Oh my goodness. Where's me gloves?

Oh there's my copper. Where was he yesterday I'd like to know? Why wasn't he at the Convention of Toolmakers at the Fishmongers Hall? There was just one little policewoman on duty. They don't take care of him properly. I always take an umbrella now to wallop any assassins. Oh, me flowers. After he'd gone in I went round the corner and there were police everywhere, stopping traffic and everything. For what? Fergie going to a fashion show. I was livid. They keep giving him all the rotten jobs. That Fergie gallivants about all over the place and Di gets all the premières. Oh well, he'll soon be out of it. They can stuff their Fishmongers Hall, he'll be in Hammersmith as snug as a bug in a rug.

She does her curtsy.

She puts a vase of flowers on the sill of the ticket window.

Oh doesn't everyone look nice. Except that blonde woman there. What does she think she's come as? Why hasn't she got a hat on? And gloves? Common as muck. They've got no manners some of them. There's only two things in life I can't abide – bad manners and cruelty to animals – except cockroaches. She's uncouth. I hope he ignores her. Oh I've come over faint. I can't believe this is happening. I'm trembling like a leaf. Look at me trembling. My knees won't take me for my curtsy. Come on Doreen. Think how *he's* feeling at the moment. On the verge of a national crisis. When he beckons I'll walk out of here and never come back. They kept me away from Danny and stopped me singing with Barry, but this time I'll find my true love. Oh it's all gone quiet.

She pokes her head out of the window.

Oh no, he's here. I can see the entourage. Oh I can't believe it. There he is, bless him. He looks so handsome. He's shaking hands with Mr Beringer. He looks a bit white round the gills. Now the Open Space man. Oh good, he's turned his back on blondie with no hat. I knew he would. Only two away now. This is it. He's coming, he's coming. Now.

Doreen curtsies and disappears behind the counter. All we can see above the counter is her hat.

Go to black.

Come up on Doreen's bedsit, that evening. Doreen is sitting in the fading light. She has a plate on the small table by her side and is drinking tea from the bone china cup.

How's your cake – all right? It's a nice bit of sponge I think, although I says it as shouldn't. Don't put too much in your beak at once.

We see that she is talking to the bird.

It'll keep all right in a tin. It was the curtsy that did it . . . I hadn't reckoned with the counter . . . I shouldn't have gone so low. By the time I stood up he'd gone. Gone out of the door . . . Well, he couldn't hang around . . . Could he? . . . I suppose . . . No, he couldn't.

Perhaps it's just as well . . . It's just as well he didn't see me. He might have been tempted. Who am I to lead him astray? Make him betray his trust? I mean, I'm relieved in a way. I don't want to break up the Royal Family. I could never have been happy knowing I'd done that. And rock the Throne. Look at the Duchess of Windsor. She never lived it down. I don't want to end up all alone in Paris having my jewels auctioned after I'm gone.

I'll press these flowers in my scrap-book to remind me of this day. It's like a fairy-tale. He passed within four feet of me. This has been the happiest day of my life.

Now I can put Danny and Barry back again. And let's put up a new one of Philip.

She looks through her Royalty magazine.

Oh, this is lovely – with the Pope. *Il Papa* it says, isn't that nice. Hasn't he got a lovely face, the Pope?

Doreen contemplates the Pope's picture as she sings.

> All the time I thought there's only me
> Crazy in a way that no one else could be.
> I would have given everything I owned
> If someone would have said you're not alone.

Fade out.

Sandy Comes Home

The ruminations of a revenant

BARRY HUMPHRIES

SANDY STONE Barry Humphries

Produced by Fiona Finlay
Directed by David Bell
Designed by Rochelle Selwyn
Music by Bill Connor

(This is the full version of Sandy Comes
Home *from which the television monologue
was abridged.)*

We are in a Melbourne suburb. The camera takes us along a line of houses to a street sign. Close up on the sign, then we move up the pathway of a house to the front door. In the hallway/living area we hear loud bouzouki music. Nick (the Greek buyer of the house) is up the step-ladder, painting. On the ladder is his paint-stained ghetto-blaster.

Enter his wife, heavily pregnant. She is carrying a can of beer for Nick and a roll of fabric. Nick stops painting, she hands him up his beer. She moves to the living-room and tries material at the window. She looks at the bassinet proudly. She crosses to the cot. Nick, still drinking, crosses over and appraises it with her. He approves, taps her bottom. He picks up ghetto-blaster and they leave the room. Bouzouki music fades.

Sandy appears in his armchair. As he looks at a lamp in the living-room it flickers as though Sandy is sending it a message.

I didn't want to come home. Our house, Kyora, 36 Gallipoli Crescent, Glen Iris, has been bought by a delightful multi-cultural Greek ethnic minority couple. At the auction the bidding got pretty fierce. At one stage of the game we thought our house might be knocked down to a couple of boat people. But in the end the multi-culturals won. Not that, when you've passed away as I have, you can ever be sure who's going to live in your house and, by the same token, when you buy an established residence, you can never be sure if the deceased occupant has granted you vacant possession. But I didn't want to come home . . . It's a funny story. After I passed away . . . caught the ferry . . . jumped the twig . . . was gathered . . . had my last cup of Milo . . . my wife, my widow, Beryl, decided to put this place on the market so she could move up to a condominium in the sun at Surfer's Paradise. So she threw a lot of my left-off effects into a tea-chest, dropped them off at the Holy Trinity Voluntary Helpers Bring and Buy Thrift Shop along with my favourite armchair. I took it pretty philosophically. Beryl wasn't to know I was still sitting in it. I don't know how long I was sitting in that chair in that thrift shop window either . . . I could have been there six or seven years. But one morning this little Greek mother-to-be, this little Papadopoulous woman, she came in, she fell in love with this chair, had it delivered to her new home, her new home which turned out to be my old home . . . Kyora . . . 36 Gallipoli Crescent, Glen Iris, Melbourne . . . a chance in a million. Fate

moves in a mysterious way. But I didn't want to come back. The house, the
street, everything's changed out of all proportion, since the old days before
the War when young people like me and Beryl came to live here, not that we
ever had anything against the occasional multi-cultural. Beryl always had
'Welcome' on her doormat, but that didn't mean you invited them onto the
premises. I remember before the War, she used to get all her fruit and all
her vegetables delivered by a little Chinaman, a little smiling Chinaman by
the name of Charlie O'Hoy. He used to drive his horse and cart once a week
religiously from his market garden on the Banyule Estate at Heidelberg,
behind the gasometers. He'd come up the cutting, round past Ivanhoe and
Alphington where the papermills are today. And then up by Studley Park,
up the hill past the Lunatic Asylum to the T-junction of Cotham Road and
then you go down Glenferrie Road, down past the Methodist Ladies College
on the left, over Barkers Road, along there under the railway bridge by the
Hawthorn Town Hall, up that little rise over the tram line at Riversdale
Road and then to the top of the hill, and then you go down that hill, down
past Scotch College on the right and through by Cooyong past the tennis
courts and then hard left all the way, via Gardiners Creek to Glen Iris. Quite
a long journey for the little yellow Chinaman in a horse and cart.
Particularly in view of the fact that sometimes Beryl's only requirement was
an onion. But little did we know then, before the War, that he was the thin
edge of the wedge, after the War the flood gates would open . . . now it's a
case of come one, come all. I mean the Stubbings' beautiful house, number
54, just down the road, that's been remodelled from top to bottom by a
Vietnamese couple from Vietnam by the name of Ng. Ng. That's their
name. Ng. N G is how they spell it . . . we thought at first that they might
have shortened it out of consideration for their neighbours. Shortened it to
Ng, that is to say, not from Ng. You couldn't very well do that. Well, you
could, I suppose, you could shorten it to 'G' or 'N', but we wouldn't have
expected them to do that. We were happy to meet them halfway down the
road. As far down the road as possible. Then we thought their name might
have been the first and last letters of something . . . like nothing. But you
could smell their cooking on the bowling green. Old Phyllis Prescott looked
through the fence once and she saw the Ngs sitting on the patio shelling
peas. She said she couldn't believe that they threw the peas away. They just
cook the shells. They put them on a dustbin lid with a bit of Worcestershire
sauce, then they throw in anything that moves. There was a lot of worry

when Miss Warner's cocker spaniel went missing. Luckily it turned up in the dog pound or those Ngs could have been in trouble. They could have been deported if they had had passports. But the first house in our street to actually fall into enemy hands – foreign hands – was Vi and Allan Chapman's lovely Californian bungalow directly across the road from us at number 37. We'd known Vi and Allan of course for years. We were in the tennis club with them before the War, and the bowls and the crazy whist. But latterly they'd become very elderly, we were quite concerned as to how elderly they had become, and their daughter-in-law Beverley had been trying to get them into a little flat for some years. That's the main function of a daughter-in-law – getting old people into little flats. You see they want us all on the one level, below ground level if you ask me. But Vi and Allan wouldn't budge. They clung on until the eleventh hour. They were still in the lounge room watching *Neighbours*, even after the TV had been disconnected, when the new owner Bruno Agastino and his family of eleven had their tea-chests in the driveway plus all their other appliances. But of course once they had moved into that home, it was swarming with Italians, night and day. Talk about build. They extended themselves out of all proportion. They built on the back, they built on the front, they built on the left, they built on the right: they built another storey on that home. They dug underneath the blessed place, they built on the house itself. Till it filled up the entire plot, from the right-of-way to the front fence. And it would have broken Vi Chapman's heart to see what they did to her porch. They built a balustrade across the front of the home, with fountains and statues, blessed lions, lions everywhere. It was a cement safari. They hid that front lawn. They got a rotary hoe to it, they dug up every trace of Vi's green fingers. I can remember Vi weeding that lawn before the War. And she had a beautiful lawn. She had that little silver birch and a fish pond with a bit of chicken wire over it, to stop the fish getting out. It was beautiful. These Italians ploughed the lot up, and round the back too, where she had that pin oak tree, and I remember when she bought that tree as a seedling at a Methodist Church fête before the War. And it grew into a lovely tree, it was a beautiful tree when war broke out. Well, it resisted the bulldozer for the best part of a day and in the end they got the block and tackle to it and it came down with a groan that you could hear up and down the street. And only when they were chopping that tree up, did they find the bit of rotten wood nailed onto one of the branches – all that was left of a little tree house that Neil Chapman had played in before the War. Of course, Neil was beheaded in Borneo. Some Jap with a sword said 'Kneel' and he did and that was that. Terrible to think your destiny can be in your own name. Well, we went up to see Vi and Allan in the little flat that their daughter-in-law had bought for them but by then Allan had had a major stroke and Vi was blind. Beryl never goes anywhere empty-handed though and she'd made a lovely pineapple upside-down cake that she'd got off a recipe on a label off a Golden Circle Pineapple tin. She got most of it off the label, there was a bit that stuck to the tin that she never got – but it was a lovely cake. And old blind Vi knew what it was, just by the feel of it. She said 'You've brought me a sticky cake, Beryl.' We were amazed. I mean, when you think of all the things it could have been! And then she asked Beryl a very embarrassing question. Suddenly out of the blue she said 'Beryl'. And Beryl said 'Yes'. She said 'Are those Italians looking after my beautiful garden?' I've never been more proud of my wife's diplomacy. She gave Vi a long look of reassurance – completely wasted, as it happened. She said 'They're certainly taking care of your garden, Vi.' She said 'You have nothing left to worry about there.' Oh, down the road, where the Longmires used to live, now that house has been bought by a Chinese couple. Well, the first thing the Chows did was to build the Great Wall of China up the front of the house, about a nine-foot-high fence. The neighbours can't see in, and old Doris Morrison who never misses a trick – dear old Doris Morrison, who invented Neighbourhood Watch – she can't see over the fence, so she's lost interest in life itself. She even began to neglect her meals on wheels. Little casseroles started to pile up on her doorstep. Just the opportunity her daughter-in-law was waiting for. She frog-marched Doris into a maximum security retirement village. It had all mod cons too, including little buttons on the wall that the old folk could fall against in an emergency, if they were lucky and their aim was very very good. Mind you, they had to police that a bit. If they were alive the next day they got fined. Well, that house was on the market within minutes. And then the ambulance taking Doris away nearly collided with the cars coming to view the property. And there was the daughter-in-law showing people around with the oven still warm from Doris' last batch of scones. Her dripping still hadn't set in the blue striped bowl on the windowsill. A damp Kleenex in her nightie pocket under the pillow. Her crumbs in the bed and her teeth in the kitchen. That house found a willing buyer in Doctor Farouk

Bennarrassimon, an Indian doctor and his wife who work at the University. Beryl said the wife had the brains. And she used to get around in a saki all day long. And she would always walk about four paces behind her husband, something to do with their diet. Mind you, if Beryl and I ate nothing but curry, I hope, well, we'd come to some arrangement. Then there was Lois and Theo Gosper's house. They're dead now, Lois and Theo, but we knew them as a young couple before the War in the tennis club, the bowls and the crazy whist. Their lovely Spanish mission style home has been bought by a little Greek by the name of Con Skorpios. He pioneered formal dress hire in our neighbourhood. He rents old pale green and mauve ruffled shirts to young chappies who want to be married looking like snooker players. There's a shilling in that apparently. He doesn't live there. He rents the house out to some Australian students. Funnily enough they're the only Australians now living in our street. The students don't do much: they roll their own cigarettes and have door slamming competitions. Being unemployed they all have cars. They park the cars on Lois' front lawn and I can still see little Lo before the War on her hands and knees weeding that lawn but now it looks like old photos of the Battle of the Somme. The students get up in the middle of the night and go out and slam the doors. Then they go back to bed again. They're probably on a grant to do that. The students buy all their clothes at the Bring and Buy Thrift Shop and I've recognised a couple of my cardigans and there's a beatnik punky girl with green pointy hair and a safety pin in her nose. She's got a little kiddy running around with no nappy on and a safety pin in her own nose! She wears the suit that I was married in. Mr Skorpios got himself onto the Council and is trying to change the name of the street to a Greek name like Parthenon Road, but it would be a tragedy to lose a lovely old Australian name like Gallipoli. Dot! Dot Swift! Fancy forgetting Dot swift. She was about our favourite neighbour and she was lovely to Beryl when we first came to live in this street before the war. Dot Swift was once a very fat woman. Beryl told me that before the war Dot took a 42D cup. I never knew what Beryl meant by that – I assumed that she'd once borrowed something and failed to return it, but I never realised that Beryl numbered her utensils. Anyway, she was a beautiful person and a very refined woman, Dot. She came from a very comfortably off family. She was born into a beautiful home, her parents were very comfortably off. She'd been born into a lovely house, near here. It was one of those big old period houses, with big wide verandahs, and wisteria all over the front of it, up on the hill called Braeside, and it was in Braeside Avenue, too, which I always thought was a bit of a coincidence. And she'd spent her girlhood there and then she married Wilf and came to live in Gallipoli Crescent with me and Beryl, and Vi and Allan Chapman, and Lois and Theo Gosper, and the Longs, and the Dunns, and the Greys, and the Clarks – people with real names. And then Wilf had an inoperable polyp and only then did Dot move into a tiny little flat on the recommendation of her daughter-in-law. It was a very small flat. The real estate man had hit the nail on the head when he said it was a deceptively small flat. But it had everything that opens and shuts. I mean if you wanted to open something, you had to shut something else. Anyway, it was a lovely home, for the time being, but she'd never been back to Braeside where she'd been born, because that mansion'd been . . . well, it wasn't in the family any more. Her father left it to the Church, and the Church sold it to a consortium of doctors who turned it into a private nursing home for the bewildered. It was very popular, too – the bewildered spoke very highly of it indeed. They never advertised, it was always word of mouth, one bewildered person talking to another. And in the end the word spread round the whole of the bewildered community, which is bigger than you'd think, it's enormous. It is huge, according to a bewildered spokesman. But the doctors made some improvements. They chopped down the trees, they poisoned the wisteria and they even changed its name from Braeside to Montcalm. Probably because they thought that might be a little bit less bewildering to the bewildered. Though if you looked at the gate you could see where the original name of the house had been. Oh, and they built a cream brick geriatric wing over the croquet lawn. One morning Dot was in her little flat and she had a fall. She took a bit of a tumble. Funnily enough, Jocelyn, her daughter-in-law, was there at the time having a bit of furniture valued. 'Course, she knew that when old people fall, you don't move them so she had a cup of tea and then she couldn't stand the groaning in the other room any longer. So next morning she looked up the yellow pages under Twilight, to see if she could find a nice facility for the old lady and she did. She found a nursing home only about seven streets from here, up the hill in the old part of Glen Iris – a place called Montcalm, which had been Braeside, Dot's childhood home . . . though Jossie, the daughter-in-law, I don't think ever knew that. So picture Dot Swift on the doorstep of Montcalm with nothing but what she stood up in . . . or what she'd fallen over in. She still had some family treasures but they're back at the flat, nothing that she could move into one room. Where's her ruby glass? Where's her cruet? Her credenza? Her old Ansonia clock? Her Apostle teaspoons? Her solid brass spark arrester? Her tongs, bellows and little shovel that used to dangle by the fireplace – where's that gone? Where's the doilies and the serviettes that smelt of camphor that had hardly ever been used? And the framed views of Egypt and the pianola rolls of *Flora Dora*, *Chu Chin Chow* and *The Maid of the Mountains*? Jocelyn made sure Dot was safe in the ambulance before she beckoned the house clearance people up the driveway and got the incinerator roaring. So Dot Swift is on the doorstep of Montcalm, but naturally, she doesn't recognise these big wide mosaic verandahs where she'd played as a child, because they're teeming with wheelchairs now. And how would she know the big front room where she learnt the piano as a kiddie because now it's full of little old ladies with tubes up their noses, all enjoying *Blind Date*. By one of the coincidences that only seem to happen in real life, they allocate Dot a room right at the back that had once been her nursery. But she doesn't recognise that either, because . . . well, rooms get smaller as you get older and this one really has, because they've lowered the ceilings and they've squeezed six beds into it and she hasn't seen it for sixty-seven years, anyway. But on the third day, when she comes a little bit out of the sedation, she gets a young nurse to help her to the window – costs her money, but she does – and when she looks out of that window for the first time in sixty-seven . . . what? Sixty-eight years . . . she can't believe her eyes because there, still standing, is the old peppercorn tree where her dad once fixed up a swing. It's standing in the doctors' car park now, pretty well torn to ribbons by BMWs. But the next morning, the morning nurse, who comes from Sri Lanka, and likes a Maxwell House and a king-sized mentholated St Moritz with the physio at eleven, they have a good laugh at Dot's expense. She said 'You know that new one, that Mrs Swift in 21,' she said, 'she's a character.' She said 'Do you know what she does all day long? She just stands in that window looking at the car park saying "Where's my swing? Where's my swing?" She thinks she's a budgie . . . She thinks she's a budgerigar!' I'm glad I never had a fall. I mean, you only have to trip these days for your daughter-in-law to be into the yellow pages. The world is full of elderly citizens lying on the carpet looking up at their daughters-in-law saying 'I didn't fall, I didn't fall, I like it down here. I'm just dusting the skirting boards.'

I get a lot of letters. It was a fatal day when I filled in that coupon applying for a Reader's Digest Special Offer. Beryl said 'You do that, and they'll pursue you beyond the grave.' They have. I get six letters a week . . . I've been dead six years. Beryl gets a big post but she never left a forwarding address. She was in too much of a hurry to soak up the sun in her new condominium at Surfer's Paradise. She's Beryl Lockwood now. She married old Clarrie Lockwood, and I'm glad she did. I wouldn't want her to be lonely – not living and lonely. And I'd go up there and keep an eye on her too, if the tram went twelve hundred miles. I still love a tram ride. The conductor never asks me for the fare, either – special concession for the dead. All-night buses are full of us. I won't outstay my welcome here, though . . . I didn't want to come back. Never go back. Never go back. I'll just wait until their little one arrives. It's funny that Greek couple turning this room into a nursery. Bit of a coincidence really.

Sandy stands and starts to move to the bassinet.

Beryl and I once used to call this the nursery for a bit. But I'm glad there'll be a kiddie in Kyora at last, and I'm glad . . . I'm glad Beryl didn't throw away all my bits and pieces. She used to call me a hoarder. She'd say 'You're a hoarder'. She always had a gift for words, Beryl. She'd say 'You can't take it with you' – she certainly didn't.

Sandy stands near the mantelpiece.

She hardly took anything with her. She even forgot, she forgot our wedding photo – fancy forgetting that! Still, this'll be interesting to the little new arrival – give him an idea what a married couple look like. There's a lot of my memorabilia still here– there's the pianola rolls we bought, when we thought we might be getting a pianola. And the biscuit barrel I won at Housey-Housey. My bowls trophy! Valda Clissold wanted that as a souvenir of me. Beryl said she could easily take it into town and have my name buffed off it. But Valda never came back for it – so there it is, in pride of place. They love a bit of history on their doorstep, the Greeks. Empty tin. A lock of my mother's hair – still there. Thought we'd lost that years ago. Cherished by those ethnic minorities.

Sandy moves back to armchair after replacing tin on mantelpiece.

Still, it's good for children to be brought up in a home with a few old-fashioned things scattered about. We had them, you see, when we were young. Oh, they'd say, don't dare touch that, it belongs to Nana. Or don't touch that – that *is* Nana. I remember, she had the *Pictorial Atlas*. I once looked up the word 'Aborigine'. It said original inhabitant – that would make Beryl and me a couple of Abos. So this is my Dream Time. This is my sacred tribal site.

Nick's wife fills bin with contents of mantelpiece. Sandy disappears . . . then reappears.

If that's how they treat a man's memorabilia, don't give them back the Elgin Marbles!

Fade out.

The Last Supper

CARLA LANE

TERENCE HALLIDAY Michael Angelis

Produced by Fiona Finlay
Directed by Robin Nash
Designed by Rochelle Selwyn
Music by Bill Connor

Terence Halliday is a middle-aged butcher. The play is set in his shop in Liverpool. It is a small shop, though run with obvious cleanliness and pride. At first the place is empty. We pan around silently. We see little plastic trays in the window and the bits of decorative green that have been placed around. We see the chopping board with pieces of meat waiting to be cut and prepared on it.

My divorce is coming through today. I don't know why she's done this – I'm a reasonable man. She said to me last night . . . oh we still talk, we haven't finished torturing each other yet you see. So we had a salad supper and a glass of wine – she likes salad – nuts and lettuce and things. 'Don't bother doing a proper meal,' she said, 'just a salad.' So I did. By the table on another chair I placed the box, the small cardboard grocery box. When she arrived she casually dropped her handbag into it. It didn't seem to mean anything to her. 'The table looks good,' she said. We sat down. So, she is watching my face, I'm watching her face. I know it, you see, I can tell what she's going to say by her face. The curious little re-positioning of her mouth, the sudden drawing back of everything, as though someone had caught her by the hair and pulled it all smooth. 'You do know, don't you Terence' (that's my name) . . . 'you do know that if you had been a different person, we wouldn't have come to this.' (*Pause.*) With the thrill of the accusation over, everything drops again, the hallmarks of life come back, little lines gather around her eyes. I found myself shouting now – 'I'll tell you something Eden' – that's her name – 'you're only happy when you're criticising me – I can see it on your face.' Then with carefully selected venom, 'you look young when you're criticising me.' (*Pause.*) She chases a walnut around her plate with a fork – you can't pick a walnut up with a fork, but she keeps doing it. Eventually it skids off the plate and I can hear the cat crunching it under the table. (*Pause.*) She's really wounded now. She doesn't like that word 'young'.

'There are some people,' she said, 'think I look younger all the time.' Aye, I thought, and I know one of them; still I wasn't going to mention that, not tonight. (*Starts placing chops.*) It's funny isn't it how we cling to familiar things – the old cardigan with the buttonholes bigger than the buttons, a certain room in the house, not always the sunniest or the most comfortable, but when you go through the door it holds you, like a lover on a railway platform – the sweet coming together of familiarity. That's how I feel (*Pause.*) about her. (*Pause.*) She bites a mouthful of lettuce, crunch, crunch. She avoids the piece of tomato because she knows that the soft bit will fall through the fork and she can't say effectively cruel things when there's a squelching noise. 'Anyway Terence Halliday,' she says, 'I've learned a lot through you, I'll choose my people in future. I won't go rushing in with my eyes closed and my legs open.' I blame it on the people she mixes with – they're obsessed with the dimensions of the ozone hole and the tampering of man with the universe. 'Where man treads, he leaves chaos,' she says. 'Our dog used to drink puddles once, you don't see dogs drinking puddles now,' she said. 'They know, that's why – they know.' 'What do they know,' I said – 'what?' She looked at me. The boiled egg was in pieces now, the only way she could get it into her mouth was to mash it with the cottage cheese – but she never mashed things – I'll say that for her. (*Pause.*) Instead she put it carefully to one side with the rest of the walnut, and she laid her fork down with the air of an artist who'd just completed a masterpiece. But her face hung like a dark curtain. 'You've got blood on your shirt,' she said, 'there, at the front.' 'It's only a spot,' I said. 'It's still blood,' she said. 'It's that holiday that did it,' I said. 'What holiday?' she said. 'That holiday – in Torremolinos.' She shifted nervously, and in her bid to seem at ease she took her bag out of the little box and searched about in it – there was the familiar sound of female paraphernalia. 'Did what?' she said. 'All this,' I said, 'all this – divorce.' She closed her bag and put it back in the box. Her hand went to the little silver dolphin brooch in her blouse. 'We're not going to go through all that again, are we? Not that saga, not that never-ending, boring epic. It's like bacteria – every time you go to it it's multiplied. The only thing left that's true is Torremolinos. All you've got to do to make it a complete figment of the imagination is to say I went to bloody Bahrain!' The little brooch fell on to her plate. She picked it up and wiped the salad cream off it. 'You've broken my brooch, now,' she said.

She never did explain who Rex was. This card came through the door one day – it said 'thank you for a lovely time, love Rex.' It was posted in Aintree, but the picture was of a beach in Torremolinos. 'Who is he?' I said. 'A friend.' 'What does he mean – a lovely time – what lovely time?' 'We talked.' 'I'm talking to people all day,' I said, 'I don't go sending them cards saying "thank you for a lovely time."' 'You're different,' she said.

He starts dressing the meat with greenery.

We were on the dessert now – summer pudding – it's her favourite. I had a hell of a job making it – I'm not a culinary man. I lined the dish with bread and I put the stewed berries in, but when I came to put the top piece of bread on, it kept sinking in the juice. I took it out of the fridge next morning and turned it out on to a plate. It looked as if a giant jellyfish had fallen from a great height. So I left it where it was and poured yoghurt all over. She likes yoghurt.

'I expect you'll get in touch with that Rex when it's all over,' I said. 'I might,' she said. 'Give him another lovely time.' 'You're bad minded,' she said – and there was a loud sucking noise as she lifted a spoonful of the pudding and dropped it into a dessert dish. 'Adultery, that's called,' I said. 'How can it be adultery – I didn't go to bed with him.' 'How do I know?' I said. 'Because I'm telling you,' she said. 'You weren't the same,' I said, 'you were never the same – not in bed you weren't – not with me.'

We ate our summer pudding silently. I'd forgotten to put sugar in it. It was so sharp that everything went out of focus for the first few minutes, but my heart was bouncing about in my chest. It was as though someone was throwing a ball from my heart to my head – boom boom, boom boom. Her face had that drawn-back look again – she was going to say something. I threw my spoon down and leapt to my feet. 'Why!' I said, 'Why!' She wiped the yoghurt off her eyebrow and looked at me steadily. There was more on her fringe but I didn't tell her. 'You're violent,' she said. Violent? 'You'd hit me if you could.' 'What do you mean if I could – I can but I don't.' 'You know what I mean,' she said. She was spitting the little berry seeds and putting them on the other plate with the boiled egg and the walnuts. 'You didn't top and tail these properly,' she said.

In songs and poems and women's magazines, they applaud mystery – man is supposedly intrigued by the distance woman puts between them. I thought about this as she got up to draw the curtains. 'People can see in,' she said. Her bangles made little bell sounds as she stretched her arms up. Her blouse lifted and I could see the mole on her back. Suddenly, the body I knew so well, the one which used to plod like a pale ghost around the bedroom, with its puckers and folds and its blotches and veins, suddenly it seemed like a secret temple – a place where only I had the right to worship. It's mine, I thought, that mole is mine.

He walks to the window to put the chops down and goes to the other end of the counter, which he starts to wipe.

I had a word with Brian, not long after Torremolinos. We were at the Conservative Club. We only joined because they have a bowls outing once a year and there was always a good game of poker going on in the back room. I had thought about resigning once, especially after the Keith Jameson affair. We had this Committee Meeting to compose his obituary. Alan Murdoch, the Chairman – I never liked him, he laughed a lot – he suggested that we had tasteful memorial service cards printed in gold on white, and in the meantime, we put a notice on the Club board – something like 'We regret the sudden passing of our dear friend and colleague,' followed by his name and some useful dates and the Club logo.

I found myself pointing out to them that Keith Jameson wasn't dead yet. 'No, but he is dying, we do know that,' said Paul Draker, 'and it takes at least two weeks to get these things printed.' Stanley Cox coughed. His belly shook against the table, making all the drinking glasses clink. 'It's called planning, Terence,' he said. (*Pause.*) Keith Jameson died three months later. The memorial cards had faded a bit by then, but all they had to do with the board notice was rephrase it and leave out the word 'sudden'.

Anyway, we sat there, Brian and me, by the bar. He drew in the froth off his beer – it settled on his moustache as usual. I could never talk when it was there and he never wiped it away. He just let it snap, crackle and pop all round his mouth. So I waited until it had played itself out and then I said, 'They seem to have enjoyed themselves, Eden and your Stella – in Torremolinos.' 'Oh aye,' he said, 'she wants to go again next year.' 'Don't you mind?' I said. 'Why should I mind?' he said. His eyes were fixed on the barmaid's chest. It marauded unchecked beneath her sweater, and when she leaned forward I felt completely outwitted by it. 'Well,' I said, 'it leaves room for temptation, doesn't it? – you know – little physical skirmishes.' 'Well, why not?' he said. 'We'd all be a sight better off if we had a few more little physical skirmishes.' I decided to study the barmaid's chest – maybe it held the answer – it lolled about shamelessly. Her mouth looked like one of those big, scarlet, silk lips you see on a Valentine card. I tried to feel something, excitement, lust, abandonment – but when she reached towards me to wipe the counter down, I felt like a man trapped in a cul-de-sac by a steam-roller. 'Anything else I can do for you love?' she said. 'Not half,' said Brian. And they all started laughing around the bar – all of them.

He moves back to the other end of the counter – collecting a roll of meat.

We were on the coffee now. We'd discussed after-life, the way sugar shines in the dark. And now she was expounding about the rain forests. 'Man doesn't care,' she said. 'If woman ruled the world, the universe wouldn't be dying.' 'Mrs Thatcher's a woman,' I said. 'She can't do it on her own, can she? It needs mothers, lovers, minders. Man goes out every day, with his briefcase and his Filofax, harming the world – while woman stops the children from running into the road.' She reeled straight into another thought. 'I notice the one experiment the scientists aren't doing – they're not making it possible for man to have the babies, are they?' 'What good would that do?' I said. 'It would give us all something to laugh about,' she said. I picked up the milk jug. 'I don't take milk,' she said. 'You took it once,' I said, 'I remember.' 'Not since . . .' she stopped. 'Torremolinos,' I said, 'not since Torremolinos.'

I remember she had a little yellow dress, it was straight except for round the bottom, there was a frill – it used to bounce around her knees when she walked and gather around them like butterflies when she sat down. (*Pause*.) She wore it at the airport. We got there early – Brian and Stella went off to buy a camera because Stella had forgotten to bring hers and Eden wanted to use hers. 'She'll probably go to a bullfight,' she said. 'When in Spain,' I said. She looked at me for a moment and I saw something hostile reach her face, and then – 'You've got blood on your sleeve,' she said. 'It's only a spot,' I said. 'It's still blood,' she said.

We kissed for a long time before she went. Brian and Stella stood by the check-in, waiting. There was always something comfortable about them – they didn't seem to need reassurance. He kissed her cheek and patted her bottom and that was it. Eden and me needed the ritual – the 'I love you,' the 'I'll miss you,' the 'I'll call you.' She didn't call – well she did once to say they'd arrived safely. But not after that. I called the hotel a couple of times – 'How's it going?' I said. 'Wonderful,' she said, 'it's just wonderful.' 'A lot of sun?' I said. 'I'm really brown,' she said. Something ran through me. All the things I was supposed to feel at the sight of the barmaid's chest, ran through me – brown – my Eden – brown. 'Have you been anywhere exciting?' I said. 'Oh, just the odd place, the odd dance – don't worry about me,' she said. 'Stella and I are always together, we're having such a laugh.'

Pause.

I never saw the yellow dress again – she said she'd left it at the hotel. I rang up from the shop one day – they said they hadn't found it – they'd searched everywhere they said. 'It was yellow,' I said, 'with a frill round the bottom.' 'Sí, Señor, I remember the dress,' he said, 'it is not here.' (*Pause.*) He remembered the dress. (*Pause. Sharpens knife.*)

I'd bought some little heart-shaped biscuits to have with our coffee – chocolate covered they were. I began to engrave her initials on some of them – you know – carve the chocolate away – making a biscuit-coloured 'E'. I did three of them, but suddenly it didn't seem right – not for a divorce. So I ate them. 'What are you going to do?' I asked, 'afterwards, I mean?' 'Oh, see what comes along I suppose.' 'No plans then?' 'Only to be happy – I insist on being happy – I might travel.' My stomach somersaulted. 'Oh, where?' I said as casually as I could. But already castanets and tambourines were ringing through my blood. 'Nowhere in particular, just somewhere.' He's a travelling salesman, I thought. The bastard. He was probably in Wales when she went to see her Aunty Sissy, and that strange place she started going to, some club or another, filled with dog lovers and vegans. 'Italy is nice,' I found myself saying – 'Rome.' 'Is that what you're planning?' I saw a moment's interest, her right shoulder moved slightly – it always did that when she was feeling unsure of things. I adopted an enigmatic air. 'Who knows,' I said. I reached for a heart-shaped biscuit just as she reached for a walnut. We put them in our mouths simultaneously and we both laughed. It was the first time we had laughed together for years. Her eyes and teeth and skin turned into stars.

She stirred her coffee, then pushed it away. 'You've put milk in it,' she said. 'Sorry,' I said. 'You always do that.' 'Sorry,' I said. 'Milk is cruel,' she said. Normally I would ask why – why is milk cruel? And she would say something like, 'Because cows and calves are separated and they grieve for one another.' Then I would tell her that she was fast turning into a crank and she would shout something like, 'If cranks ruled the world it would be a safer place.' And I would shout something like, 'So what is it eh? Who's going to rule the world – cranks or women? Make up your mind.' But I decided to stay enigmatic and profound. 'Everything's cruel,' I said – 'you are cruel – I am cruel – life is cruel.'

Final cutting of meat.

Our coffee had gone cold. She reached over and lifted the skin from mine and delivered it to the little pile of nuts and eggs and berry seeds on her plate. 'I'll be a sad man tomorrow,' I said. 'You sad,' she said, 'I don't associate you with being sad.' It occurred to me that this great pain, which I had carried around with me since Torremolinos, had not even occurred to her. I wanted to say: of course I get sad you silly bitch, I cart sadness around with me, the way you cart your bloody handbag round – but I didn't – I kept silent. The cat jumped from behind the table into the box. She reached for her bag to make room for him. I thought she might notice the box this time but she didn't. Then she said suddenly, 'Rex always says that . . .' she stopped. It wasn't the word 'Rex' that threw me – it was the word 'always' – Rex – always – this means often, I thought. This means, more than once, many times. It had a comfortable, domestic sound to it. The tennis match began in my chest again but I said calmly, 'Go on, Rex always said.' I was reminded of the saying, 'even a fool knows when harm has been done', as she added warm syrup to her voice, 'What I mean by always, is – he said it once – the one time I spoke to him.' 'In Torremolinos,' I said. 'Yes, in Torremolinos.' 'Not Aintree, where the card came from?' 'No, not Aintree where the card came from.' 'You didn't ever see him after you got back – you didn't ever see him in Aintree?' 'No, I never did.'

It was time to play my final card – tomorrow we would be divorced – there would be no point. I looked at her for a long time. I think I knew what it was like to be the snake gazing at the rabbit before the kill. 'What about the cardboard box?' I said. 'The one which you brought some groceries home in – the one which had written on it "Pearson's Groceries – Aintree". This box!' She looked at it blankly – then at me. And she said, ever so quietly, 'It was a little shop next to . . .' 'His place?' I said. 'Or was the shop his place?' 'It was nowhere near his place,' she said. 'It *was* in Aintree?' I said. 'Oh yes,' she said. 'It *was* in Aintree.'

Her honesty was worrying me. I was losing track of the attack. Then, as if to put me back on the road, she said, 'You kept that box? Where?' 'In the loft.' 'Why?' 'Evidence.' 'Of what?' 'Your affair.' 'It wasn't an affair – it was a friendship.' 'Thank you for a lovely time – you call that friendship?' 'We thought alike.' She leapt to her feet. 'Oh God, not all this again, not all this.' She picked up her bag. I'd lost contact with charisma and subtlety now. I had to get things straight. Everything had to be tidy. I followed her across the room and I caught her arm. 'You think you're the only one who suffers, don't you? But what about me. My wife went away on a holiday – girls together she called it – a good giggle – and I never saw her again. All that came back was this thing, this monster, this . . .'

She stared at me and she said, deliberately, without a blink, 'He was a vegetarian, that's all – we thought alike – it was a friendship – I had coffee with him in Aintree once, that's all.' 'Oh, was that the lovely time?' I said, 'it doesn't take much to please him does it?' 'We talked about . . .'

'Acid rain, pollution, insecticide, healthy living – all that crap I suppose.'

Suddenly a great passion entered her voice – 'It wasn't about healthy living, it was about – *living* – being allowed to live . . . not being chopped up.'

She made a little gesture with her hand as if to wipe the blood spot off my shirt. I don't know why she did it – you can't tell with women can you?

Then she walked away.

He starts to place meat on tray.

I talked to Brian about it – I told him everything. I didn't even wait for the froth around his moustache to evaporate, I launched straight into it.

Pause.

Oh he listened, but he didn't understand. People just don't understand. 'For Christ's sake, Terence,' he said, 'not Torremolinos again. Why don't you leave go? After all, it was nearly twenty years ago.'

I don't know why she went. I'm a reasonable man.

He crosses to window with tray and opens blind.

Fade out.

Ginger

BOB LARBEY

GINGER George Cole

Produced by Fiona Finlay
Directed by Guy Slater
Designed by Rochelle Selwyn
Music by Bill Connor

Ginger is in his sixties. He is fairly spry in his movements but his hair is thinning and grey. The play is set in his small, one-bedroomed flat in Worthing. The flat is neat enough. There is not a lot of furniture, but what there is is modern. There are no signs of memorabilia. Ginger is cleaning his suede shoes with a wire brush. He wears smart trousers, a clean white shirt and a rather snazzy bow tie. A blazer is laid over an armchair and a cardboard box is on the table.

'Brothel creepers' they used to call suede shoes. I can't imagine why. It seems to me that if a man's tendencies led him to a brothel, he wouldn't want to *creep* in. No, he'd want to walk in properly, confident in where he was and what he desired. I will admit they draw the feet a bit though, suede shoes. But they are smart.

He finishes cleaning his shoes.

There.

He puts the brush away and goes to look at himself in the mirror.

It seems to me that when you reach an age of . . . well, let's say maturity, you have to be honest with yourself. 'Mirror mirror on the wall, who is the fairest of them all?' I'd take myself for ooh, middle fifties.

Ginger opens the cardboard box and takes out a ginger wig.

But with this . . .

He settles it on top of his head. It is not the best wig ever made and is a rather violent ginger colour. He strikes a pose, but then leans forward to look more closely.

There is a sand meeting the sea effect here and there, but who's to look closely any more?

My own colour this used to be – perhaps a shade less ginger. It's like buying a suit. You sometimes look at it in the open air and it's a shade brighter than it looked in the shop. Still 'Ginger' I always was called. Mary, my second wife, wouldn't have it – made me sound like a cat, she said. Alexander she used to call me – not even Alex. But then, as I found to my cost, Mary wasn't an 'Alex' sort of person – certainly not a 'Ginger' sort of person. 'There's a time and a place for everything, Alexander,' she used to say. An overstatement. We ended up never finding the time or the place for anything, let alone everything.

Ginger puts on his blazer and looks at himself in the mirror, adjusting the handkerchief in his top pocket.

Yes, middle fifties at most. I've stayed slim, that's a lot to do with it, and I've always been limber. The only very slight physical disability I have is that I can't get my right arm quite so high over my head as the left. Then, it hardly shouts 'Disability' from the roof tops. I mean, at the end of the day, how often does one put both arms in the air? I suppose if I were involved in a hold-up it might notice, but that's not high on the list of probabilities.

They did have a hold-up at the Leisure Centre once. That was before I worked there. I was in the hut on the Pitch and Putt then. It wasn't much of a success, the hold-up. The hold-upper . . . is that right? Can't be up-holder can it? No. The hold-upper dashed into reception at such a lick that he skidded on the tiles and knocked himself out on the vending machine. Apparently it's the only time that machine's ever delivered black coffee with sugar correctly.

It's all right, the Leisure Centre. I'm not keen on the smell of chlorine in the baths, but that's more than compensated for by the badminton girls. Gives them a sort of a glow, playing badminton. I usually manage a trip or two through the hall when the badminton girls are there. 'Look out,' they say, 'here comes Ginger!' Then they all stop playing and watch me walk through. It's all very good-natured.

Ginger looks out of the window.

I don't really know why I stay down here really. Or perhaps I do. What's in Scotland for me nowadays? Familiar accents, forgotten places and two ex-wives going on and on about maintenance.

Ginger looks at his watch, then picks up a printed card from the table.

'Free introductory invitation to the Over-Sixties Club.' It came with the newspaper.

Young Norman at the Leisure Centre would make one of his totally witless jokes about that. 'Trust you to go because it's free, Ginger!' Norman's a joke in himself, though he's too vain to know it. Flashy – always leaping about in his track suit, with his sun-bed tan and whiteemulsioned teeth. I know for a fact he stuffs tissues down the front of his trousers. We walked past a crowd of the badminton girls today and you could hear them giggling all the way down the corridor. They certainly weren't giggling at me. No, I'm going to have a look at this club because . . . well, you never know do you? I have the odd free evening to spare and if I don't like it, I won't go back, it's as simple as that. Anyway, I'll just see what it's like. They'll probably think I'm too young anyway. If I don't like it, I won't go back. So, raincoat or not? No. Makes you look shapeless, a raincoat. I think I'll walk, but not along the Front. It can get a bit windy along the Front.

Ginger takes a last look at himself, then goes out of the flat.

Go to black.

Come up on Ginger's flat. Night. Ginger lets himself in. He has a somewhat stunned air about him.

My God, I've seen more life on a fishmonger's slab.

He goes into the kitchen and comes back with a can of beer and a glass. He sits and pours the beer.

I should have been warned when I first walked into the place. There's a kind of alcove just inside the door, with pegs for coats and hats. I have never seen such a variety of woolly hats in all my life. I am not a knitting man, but I swear there was every pattern there that's ever been invented. You could have made a decent bonfire out of the walking sticks. Three walking-frames – parked very neatly I must admit. If they had registration plates like cars, it could provide jobs for a number of old people, delivering them from the factory to the showroom. Of course, they'd have temporary plates on them then. You'd see all these old guys with the temporary plates under their arms, trying to hitch a lift back to the factory from the first walking-frame that came along. It's not an unamusing thought, but when I voiced it to Mr Wendell, he looked at me as though I'd just stepped out from an alien space-ship. Mr Wendell met me as I entered. He glides, Mr Wendell, that's the only word for it. His legs move so fast he looks as though he's travelling across the floor on wheels. I assume he has a rank or title of some sort – he seems to run things. But if he has a rank or title I never heard it, I think he just assumes you know.

'Come in, come in, Mr Leggatt,' he says. 'Don't stand on formality. Formality is a rude word in our club. Call me Phil.' Funny that, because the only thing I heard anyone call him all evening was 'Mr Wendell'.

'Here's a new boy – Mr Leggatt,' he shouted, which produced the longest stare from twenty pairs of eyes that I've ever been subjected to. Stunned I suppose they were – probably couldn't believe I was old enough to join. My, they were an old bunch. Mr Wendell would insist on introducing me to every single one of them – a succession of arthritic hand-shakes, looks of amazement from rheumy eyes and a lot of names that I couldn't take in. They all sat round the edge of the room like the cushions on a snooker table.

Well, the introduction took so long that by the time I arrived back at the point I'd started from, it was time for coffee and biscuits. Two of the ladies helped Mr Wendell. Powderhall sprinters they were not, so that took up another twenty minutes. I was so overcome by the excitement of it all that I forgot to eat my biscuit. 'We have a kitty,' said Mr Wendell, 'but as you're the new boy, have this one on the house.'

There was conversation of sorts, dominated, it seemed, by medical matters. I did manage to steer one chap onto politics and whether Harriet Harman has better legs than Edwina Currie, but it didn't last. Before I knew it, we'd somehow got onto the subject of hip replacements.

Then we played Bingo. 'We love our Bingo, Mr Leggatt,' said Mr Wendell. 'Do we?' I thought, but I played anyway. Five pence a card it cost, and the prize was 50p.

Not to put too fine a point on it, but the evening was beginning to pall and I was considering slipping away when Miss Probert arrived. Now there, so far as I can see, is the only reason I shall ever go back. Not a member, Miss Probert. She helps Mr Wendell, but usually comes later because of her father. Not in the first flush of youth – maybe fifty, but a fine, curved woman with dark hair and slim ankles. Her hand-shake was warm and soft and I don't think I'm entirely wrong in thinking that it lingered just a while longer than formality decrees.

She seemed to bring some life with her as well, Miss Probert. Some of the old people became positively animated, and there was laughter – everywhere that Miss Probert moved there was laughter.

The highlight of the evening was what Mr Wendell described as 'Tripping the light fantastic'. Fantastic it certainly was not and the tripping was mostly of the accidental sort. And the tunes on that tape of his – a large number of what he chose to call 'Novelty numbers'. They began with *The Chicken Song*, which I considered an insult to even the intelligence gathered there. But away they went, flapping their arms and clucking obediently. I chose not to participate in that particular débâcle. There's a lot of arm-waving goes on and I didn't want Miss Probert to notice that I can't get my right arm so high above my head as my left arm. I did make the mistake of joining in some absurd dance about Simple Simon, but as that contained even more arm-waving than the chicken thing, I withdrew smartly.

Interestingly enough, Miss Probert asked me to dance several times, but I declined. I'd decided to wait for a quick-step. I should say, in all modesty, that the quick-step is a speciality of mine.

In the meantime, on they went, 'Tripping the light fantastic'. There was a slow-motion Hokey-Cokey which seemed to consist of putting your left foot in and then seeing if you could get it out in time to get it back in again in time to shake it all about. Well of course they couldn't and the music ended long before they did.

There was a non-novelty waltz and, against my better judgement, I was persuaded to take part by Mr Wendell's cry of, 'Now come along boys – don't make the girls dance with each other all evening!' I found myself attempting to steer the deaf lady round the floor. Conversation was naturally restricted but unhappily she attempted to compensate by humming the tune. Without being unkind, I have the feeling that she was tone deaf long before she went deaf.

There weren't enough 'boys', of course, so several of the 'girls' did have to dance together. Two, of more ample proportion, had to lean on each other for support. They looked remarkably like a pair of Sumo wrestlers locked in combat. They didn't cover much of the floor, but every so often they managed to gather some momentum and launch into a few steps. I've got a very nasty scuff down the back of one of my shoes where I failed to take sufficient evasive action.

But then came a quick-step and who should I find presenting herself – yet again – as my partner but the delectable Miss Probert. I took her in my arms and swept her at least twice round the floor before anybody else could lever themselves out of their chairs. Strangely, Miss Probert was not the excellent dancer I would have taken her for. She certainly wasn't up to some of my trickier steps, with the result that I trod on her feet a few times. 'Let's slow it down a little Mr Leggatt,' she said, so I settled for a simpler version which she managed much better. It suited me too because I was able to hold her closer, which was an extremely pleasurable sensation. We didn't manage too much in the way of conversation because I had to give an amount of concentration to steering my way past the Sumo wrestlers and various others.

We didn't get another dance in, although I got the distinct impression that she'd have liked to.

The evening concluded soon after that when Mr Wendell made some feeble jokes about wrapping things up before the police were called in.

I offered to walk Miss Probert home, but as she has a car and lives in the opposite direction anyway that didn't come to anything.

Outside, it reminded me of an infants' school at the end of the day. Nearly everybody was met – sons and daughters presumably, who all seemed to be driving Volvo Estates. One group, including the Sumo wrestlers, were picked up in a Mini-van with 'St Marks' on the side. What 'St Marks' is, I have no idea. I'd sooner not think about it actually, but they were still loading as I walked away.

I had some fish and chips on the way home at a place rejoicing in the name of 'Fisherama'. There's a very attractive Greek girl who's usually in there, but apparently she'd been called into the back for something. You'd expect the fish to be fresh, living by the sea, but it never seems to be.

So – conclusion. Marks out of ten. The Over-Sixties Club – one, and that's being generous. Miss Probert – ten. I'm not a fool. I realise that she must go out of her way to make a new member welcome, but there's a bit more to it than that, I know there is. The thing is though, if I'm to pursue our relationship, I'll have to go back. But changes will have to be made. 'Gingering up', that's what it needs, and Ginger is the man to do it. They *think* old, that's the trouble. Well, we'll put a stop to that next week. A bit of ginger is what they need, and a bit of Ginger is what they're going to get!

Go to black.

Come up on Ginger's flat. Night. The door opens and Ginger comes in. He is distinctly out of sorts and defensive. He limps and his wig is awry. He goes into the kitchen and comes back with his can of beer and his glass.

You can misjudge people. There they all were when I first arrived, sitting round the walls again. This time I voiced what I'd thought the week before.

'Do you know something,' I said, 'you look like the cushions on a snooker table sitting there like that.' Nothing – not a titter. Tell a lie, I did get one response, Mr Haseldine I believe – one of the walking frames. 'Stephen Hendrey,' he says, 'comes from Scotland.' 'Yes?' I said. 'Yes,' he said and that was the end of that.

Cajoling having failed, I took action. 'Come on,' I says, 'let's gather these chairs round. Let's socialise.' I even tried to move one or two but it was like trying to prise limpets off a rock.

'Mr Wendell likes us here to start with,' says one old girl in an awful puce cardigan. 'Do *you* like it here to start with?' I said. No answer. One old guy did stand up and I thought I'd made some sort of bridgehead, but he only wanted to go to the lavatory.

Then in bustles Mr Wendell on his wheels. 'Sorry to be late boys and girls,' he says, 'managerial conference at the Library.' Managerial conference! There's only five of them work there. 'Anyway,' he says, 'enough of me. Let's play our beloved Bingo.'

'Let's not,' I says, and you could have heard a pin drop.

Managerial conference or not, the only response that came to Mr Wendell was to stand there with his mouth open. 'Let's not play Bingo,' I says, pressing home the advantage. 'Let's do something livelier – something with a bit more ginger to it. I know. Let's play "Stations" – that's always good for a laugh.'

'I am not familiar with "Stations",' says Mr Wendell – 'and quite frankly, I doubt that anyone else is.' He made it sound like anybody else in the entire world. Well, I was not about to be put off that easily, so I explained the rules. You all sit round in a circle, and each of you calls yourself a station, like St Pancras or Paddington or whatever. One person stands in the middle. Then you have a caller with a list of the stations that people have called themselves. He calls out the names of two stations and those two people have to try and change seats before the one in the middle gets into one of them. There's a supplementary rule. Any time he likes, the caller can call, 'All change!' and everybody has to change seats while the one in the middle tries to get a seat of his own.

It's a great game. I mean, if the caller calls 'All change!' several times running, it's absolute chaos.

'This club,' says Mr Wendell, 'is a democracy and if it is the will of the members to play your little games . . .' He lets the dots at the end of his sentence trail away into infinity. To be honest, I thought I'd lost the day, but who should pipe up but the old girl in the puce cardigan? 'I played "Stations" when I was a girl,' she says, and wonder of wonders, other voices piped up. 'Yes, I remember it too.' 'So do I.' 'We could try.' 'It would make a change.' The word 'change' to Mr Wendell obviously equals the mob tearing up the paving stones to make barricades, but if we were to be a mob, I was going to be the Danton. 'Aux armes les citoyens!' I didn't actually shout that but I did my best to keep the momentum going.

To tell the truth, I'm not sure I had a majority – some of them had no idea what was going on at all, but before Mr Wendell could rally the Palace Guard, I set them all to putting their chairs in a circle and picking themselves stations.

The delectable Miss Probert arrived in the middle of all this – white-bloused and blue-skirted.

'Well, Ginger,' she said, 'now what are you up to?'

I thought I detected a note of sexual challenge in her voice, but I hadn't time to pursue it because the mob were losing their head of steam and starting to quarrel about who was King's Cross and why they had three Waterloos. So I explained what we were doing and Miss Probert, bless her, smiled and said, 'What a good idea. That sounds jolly.'

So 'Stations' we played – slowly at first because Mr Wendell, ever the democrat, appointed himself caller. He called out the stations so slowly. Wat-er-loo to Padd-ing-ton. I mean, it was useless. By the time he'd got out the name of the first station, the person in the middle knew exactly which chair to rush to. Fortunately, though, he was called to the telephone – managerial presumably – and Miss Probert took over the calling. 'Stations' became the game it's supposed to be.

'Waterloo to Paddington – Euston to King's Cross – King's Cross to Euston! All change! All change! All change!' It was real good fun – noisy and happy. Not as fast as it should be because of the age of the players, naturally. I slowed myself deliberately so as not to take an unfair advantage.

The accident was not my fault. It was one of the Sumo wrestlers. As I said of the dancing, it takes some time for them to get up a head of steam, but once under way they become leviathans. It was Mr Howlett who copped it – during an 'All change'. Quite knocked the wind out of him. By this time, breath was in fairly short supply anyway, so we stopped for coffee and biscuits. Miss Probert chose to sit next to me, which I took to be a good sign.

Mr Wendell's expression as he announced it was time to 'Trip the light fantastic, boys and girls,' was one of contentment. He thought he was back on safe territory.

Oh my, he was wrong. My blood was up now, and I simply did not see why people of mature years should make fools of themselves prancing about like chickens. 'Down with chickens,' I shouted, 'Let's have *The Gay Gordons*!' To my huge delight, I got support from the hard-core survivors of 'Stations'. 'I do not have *The Gay Gordons* on my tape,' Mr Wendell smiled, making it sound like a judge pronouncing the death sentence. But I was not to be denied. There was some life there. I had produced some life.

'Don't worry, Mr Wendell,' I smiled back, 'we'll sing it ourselves!' And we did. Everybody joined in except Mr Wendell. 'Mass hysteria,' he called it afterwards.

Immodestly, I wasn't too surprised to find myself partnering Miss Probert. Her eyes shone, her hair twirled and, I have to say, my hopes rose. Unfortunately, she's just not too good with the quicker steps, Miss Probert, and I did bang her ankle a bit, so she had to go to the Ladies for running repairs. But on we all danced anyway. Oh it was grand. But then, quite suddenly, the old lady in the puce cardigan clutched her chest and started making peculiar noises. She didn't fall over. She just sat down in the middle of the floor.

Now I have to say that I do not have any formal medical training, but everyone else just stood there like dummies, so I stepped in. I've never applied the kiss of life, but I've heard about it, so I was down there in a flash.

'Dial 999 somebody – get an ambulance,' I said. Those who claimed afterwards that I said 'Fire Brigade' were obviously in shock. Anyway, I got the old lady's head down and I puffed into it, like blowing up a balloon, then sort of sucked as if picking up a dried pea with a straw. Talk about reaction! The next thing I know, the old lady is lashing out with her handbag. I wasn't ready for that, which is why she caught me. Anyway, I went sideways and banged into Mr Haseldine's knee. He did go down with a thump – a sort of clicking sound as well. 'I've broken my leg,' he says, which only served to confuse matters.

Mr Wendell just hopped about – off his wheels – saying 'Oh dear! Oh dear!' I'd have looked at Mr Haseldine's leg, but you can't be in two places at once.

I was quite pleased to see Miss Probert come back from the Ladies and see what was happening. As I've said, I have no formal medical training. 'Ginger,' she says, 'leave her alone. You've done enough.' I took that as praise, naturally, and decided to leave things to her. The ambulance came very quickly. They loaded up the old lady in the puce cardigan, still clutching her handbag, plus Mr Haseldine, with a temporary splint on his leg, and off they went.

The atmosphere had quite gone by now. Robespierre turned the mob against Danton in the end, and Mr Wendell made a very good Robespierre. You'd have thought I'd tried to strangle the old girl with my bare hands and break Mr Haseldine's leg with his own walking-frame.

Miss Probert offered to drive me home. It was pouring with rain by then. I accepted the offer of course. At least some good was coming out of that damned place.

She parked just outside the flat and we sat there for a while without saying anything.

Then she said, 'Ginger, I think you were just grand.' A good start, I thought, but I've never been one to rush things so I just smiled in what I hoped was a modest fashion. She went on in the same vein, which made very good listening. I'll be honest, I can stand flattery.

But it might be best if I didn't go back to the club, she suggested, at least for a while.

'A bit too much for them?' I asked, and she nodded.

Well I could see what she meant. I was too young. She smiled at that, and I thought this an appropriate moment to move the conversation on to more personal matters, so I enquired when and where we might see each other again.

She looked quite blank, so I repeated the enquiry. 'Ginger,' she said, 'are you asking me to go out with you?' Why the surprise? Of course I was.

She said, 'I'm forty-six years old.' 'And very well preserved too,' I told her. She shook her head slowly and looked . . . shocked. I have to say, shocked. I couldn't make it out. What happened to 'You were grand, Ginger' and all the other flattering things she'd said? Had she not meant them? I pressed her on that. I had to. Maybe I shouldn't, because she gave a small sigh, said 'Very well then' and explained. Her appreciation, she said, was for my efforts to liven up the club a bit – even if things did go slightly amiss. That was all. 'You're a fine, spirited old man, Ginger,' she said, 'but you and I – it's out of the question.'

Well, there only seemed to be one response to that kind of nonsense, so I leant across to kiss her. I never got there. She gave me such a push in the chest she nearly knocked my wig off. 'You're old enough to be my father,' she said. 'Then I bid you good night, Miss Probert,' I said, with as much dignity as I could muster. Not very much to be truthful, because my wig was crooked and for some reason my leg had stiffened up from playing 'Stations'.

'Old man', she called me.

Suddenly, Ginger takes off his wig and limps to the mirror to look at himself.

Well are you?

He looks more honestly at himself than he probably has for years, feeling the texture of his skin. He looks almost distressed.

Go to black.

Come up on Ginger's flat. Next day. Ginger is on the telephone. His wig is still off.

Of course, thank you Miss Probert.

He puts the telephone down.

The old lady in the puce cardigan died on the way to hospital. Bad luck that. It was her heart. She should have taken it easier. She was on her own apparently, so Miss Probert thought it would be . . . well . . . seemly if the club turned out for the funeral. A kind thought, but I don't know if I'll go. Miss Probert left me her number and I said I'd phone back before Friday. I never feel comfortable at other people's funerals and when all's said and done I hardly knew the old girl. I don't really see why Miss Probert should ask me.

A wonderful thought comes into his head.

Just a minute. Of course! I pressed too hard, that's what it was. After all, a spinster of forty-six might not have very much experience in such matters. That's it! It wasn't a rebuff – it was more her not wanting to be rushed.

I mean, let's face it, Miss Probert has no real reason to invite me to the funeral, unless the real reason is that she wants to see me again. It's a somewhat odd way of going about it, but then . . . with not very much experience in these matters . . . I won't let her know that I know.

I'll be discreet. No, if she wants things between us to proceed at a gentler pace, that's fine. If you want to make the running in your own way, Miss Probert, you go ahead. I'm willing.

Much cheered, Ginger stands up. He puts his wig on and looks at himself in the mirror.

Things are looking up, Ginger! Let's have another dance!

Ginger limps cheerfully towards the bedroom, humming The Gay Gordons.

Fade out.

Some Enchanted Evening

JOHN SESSIONS

BOBBY BUFFET John Sessions

Produced by Fiona Finlay
Directed by Sharon Miller
Designed by Rochelle Selwyn
Music by Bill Connor

We are in a New York apartment, carefully but inexpensively decorated and full of well-displayed awards. There is a suggestion that these aren't exactly first-rate. Bobby, a rather tense man in his thirties, is ironing. As with many musicians and certain Americans his clothing is subtly out of date. Not quite seventies but clearly early eighties. His manner is precise, his tone sardonic, confidential and potentially venomous. He sighs tetchily and moves over to record player, lifts arm off the record.

Forget the guy who's singing. Think about the one who actually sat down and wrote that. 'Half a pound of tuppeny rice, half a pound of treacle. That's the way the money goes, pop goes the weasel'. That's not a lyric, that's witchcraft, for God's sake.

He crosses to the piano and shuffles through some sheet music, reading lyrics at random.

Do you think an American would sing about being a weasel or a bag of cereal? Has to be a crazy person. A crazy person like me because I'm actually going to where they write this stuff. The land where the song refuses to shine. So why am I going? I'm going because I'm a professional. Remember that one. I mean yesterday morning I got summoned by his holiness. 'Bob, hi, I'm taking *Fly me High* to London so go check the show for loose screws, okay?' (*Pause.*) Not 'Can I frisbee something past you, Bob?' or 'Hey, Bob, how does this light your fire?' The bone was already flying through the air and Bonzo here had to make with his back legs and fetch. Bonzo was hanging loose though, maybe because I could hear what Jack was really saying. 'Bobby, save my life.' And that's why it gradually occurs to Jack he's talking to Mr Shit-together. I let the wall clock tick a bit just, you know, to consolidate my space, and then I struck up. 'This show, Jack,' I said, 'why are you taking it to London?' 'They'll love it, Bob,' he said. 'The West End will go blue banana ape shit over it. It's a universal story.' 'Universal,' I said. 'A window cleaner who wants to become a pigeon – it's quintessential New York. What you don't seem to grasp, Jack, is that music is meaningless to these people. If you think I exaggerate, I suggest you check out a Vaughan Williams sea shanty.' Jack has no choice. He has to conjure up Satan. Satan disguised as a goldfish in a Three Stooges wig, that is. He said, 'You've got to face it, Bob, he's the musical phenomenon of our

time. Broadway was dying and he got on there and pumped its chest.'
'Jack,' I said, 'I don't care how many New Yorkers line up to watch that
stuff – and I stress "watch" because a guy warbling parlour songs in a
Hallowe'en mask does not a musical make. But *Fly me High* does, so why do
you want to ship it off to weasel-land?' I've got to wait now till the cigar gets
lit. 'Nobody's forcing you to go, Bob. You just look like you need the
money.' His exact words. Nine years I've been his musical midwife and he
talks to me like I'm Hymie the help-out. Contempt should be seen and not
heard, but there's a time and place for everything. 'Jack,' I said, 'you're the
one who needs the money. I just need music. But I use it to make your
dreams come true.' Then I got up, went out, and bought myself a suitcase.

Go to black.

*We are in the bedroom of a dowdy hotel in North London. Coffee and cream
flock wallpaper and sadly unoriginal prints. There is a single bed with a
candlewick cover upon which music paper is chaotically spread. Bobby is on the
telephone.*

I have turned it on and I am still cold . . . The knob?

He taps the mouthpiece with it.

You're listening to it . . . I don't know why it broke off, maybe you should
ask it . . . There's nothing you can do tonight . . . So I just sit here with
icicles hanging off my pecker till someone comes and chips me out. I'm a
musician, for Chrissakes, not a mastodon . . . It's a prehistoric elephant . . .
Yes, and I'm going to stay pissed off till you do something . . . You'll get
someone to fetch up a what? . . . a bar fire. I see. Well, why not go totally
medieval: lace my goblet with hemlock and dump me in the plague wagon.

He slams down the telephone.

Have you ever heard of the Talisman Hotel? In Pancras Road? 'You'll like it,
Bob, it's only a stone's throw from the theatre.' I don't know what stone
Jack's throwing. If Wonderwoman tried it, she'd break her goddam
wonder-shoulder. Jack's staying in Browns. Just off Piccadilly. So, no
stone-throwing for him, he just drops them off the window ledge.

A brief pause. He sits on chair.

Oh, there's no piano here. At the Talisman. The musical director has no piano. Not to speak of. He does have a sort of alfresco harpsichord in the guests' lounge. An upright apparition with thumb tacks in the hammers: a real godsend. I have to rewrite *entire* numbers. I have three new principals who have seventeen days to hit the spot. I'm not kidding, we're talking the laying on of hands. And if I'm the miracle worker then Kurt Conklin has got to be my Helen Keller. Today, we're out there. You know, in melody's graveyard. The chorus goes (*Sings.*) 'Hi there, fly me high there, in the sky there, fly me high.' Then they stop. There's a spunky little oboe tune and then Kurt is meant to go 'Wo-oh there. So let's go there' in D major. *D major.* If music be the food of love then D major has got to be a teething ring, but do you think Kurt can hit it? (*Pause.*) Jack's choice, of course. 'But, Bob, when he smiles he looks like Chuck Norris.' How can you reason with a man who can say a thing like that? You think I'd be here if he'd told me that at Kennedy? Which brings me to Alison. We're about to board; Jack's taking a last lingering look through the pornography when he thinks it's time I heard that the leading lady is now a Brit. Surely I'd seen her Hedda Gabler on P.B.S. That'd be the Hedda Gabler with the top C, top F and four-part harmony, wouldn't it, Jack? (*Pause.*) I've been a doll with this kid. Believe me, an absolute doll. Well, this morning . . .

Bobby's voice trails away in disbelief.

'Alison,' I said, 'have you ever heard of syncopation?' 'Yes, Bobby,' I should just mention she has her back to me, 'but I've never heard of you.' I wait till she has the pissing courtesy to turn round, blasting me with all the authority of her twenty-three years. 'Well Alison,' I said, 'I hope you haven't heard of Elaine Stritch because if she'd heard what you'd just said to me, you'd be in traction.' Jack's enthusiasm for her borders on the certifiable. He thinks she sings like Marlene Dietrich. At least we agree on something.

The only guy keeping me the right side of a restraining order was Bubs Rainbird. I mean we had everything. Tone, pitch, charm you could bake with. Oh, he's on the plane home now, of course. 'It's nothing to do with "macho", Bob. It's just that Bubs is giving us blurs where we need definition.' (*Pause.*) So, tomorrow, I go back to the foot of Mount Sinai with Simon. Simon Tomkinson. While Bubs flies home annihilated, Simon will be giving us all the pazazz you only get doing a cute haircut movie set in British India.

But Simon wasn't Jack's idea. Let's be fair to Jack. Simon was Simon's idea. The other Simon. Simon the director. Simon the director was Jack's idea. It's his first musical. 'It's amazing, Bobby, isn't it, that it's my first musical?' No, Simon. Not really. But it might be if it was your second.

Go to black.

Come up on Bobby in his hotel room. It's about ten days later. He looks tired and harassed but is making a valiant effort to trim his moustache. He finishes doing this before turning to the camera.

One week. That's what I've got. One week to turn water into wine. Or, in Alison's case, whining into singing. So I guess it comes as no surprise that Simon the director should do something spectacular. Just after this morning's coffee break – Hitler's dead in his bunker but we're still on powdered milk – Simon decided to focus on the love scene just before the interval. That's between Kurt and Alison who have, of course, fallen in love. If I say Dick Powell and Ruby Keeler on nerve gas, you've just about got the picture. We didn't, naturally enough, 'focus' on the duet which has been focus-free since what seems my early childhood. Before I could begin distracting people with the music, Simon has to 'root the reality'. This meant bending over the two of them with his nose hovering between their mouths, and you've really got to hand it to him because Kurt's halitosis could bring down a B52. Alison can bask in it all day but I'm talking like this should surprise me. At last they got to the bit where Kurt had to get up and release the pigeons. (*Closes his eyes.*) Well, he couldn't just stand up. Right? He had to sort of breach like Moby Dick, smacking Simon's chin with the top of his stupid ginger head. Instantly the air was ionised with concern. Brits everywhere. Heads out of holes. 'Are you all right, Simon?' Heads coming down ropes. 'Simon, what happened?' Just for a moment – the wrong moment of course – they looked like *Anchors Aweigh*. Well, that was where Pontius here reached for the hand towel. I said 'excuse me' to the rapidly assembling intensive care unit and went in search of liquid milk.

When I got back to the theatre, I was confronted with a kind of romantic tableau. Simon's head was wedged like Excalibur in Alison's lap while the stage manager was squinting down his throat. He said, 'I don't know, Si, it's really hard to say.' He could say that okay because he said it again. After he'd said it five times, I thought I'd better take a look myself before I blacked out. Kurt was looking too but it was worth playing Siegfried to the dragon of his halitosis to discover what was wrong. Or, rather, right. Simon had bitten his tongue. Not quite in half, but near enough to convince me of the existence of God whose stand-in, as it happened, was on the scene by now. 'Looks pretty bad, Jack.' I said. You know, Jim Kildare. And he said 'Yes, Bob, he'll just have to communicate by writing on a slate.' A *slate*? You give Beethoven a slate, you want to hear everything he's got cooking, but Simon? We-don't-need-to-do-that-bit-again-do-we-can-you-stop-the-piano-playing-Simon? That was it. I just blew. Simon was a dumb asshole, possibly the dumbest. And what had happened had simply been the universe hinting at just how dumb that actually was. I'd had it with him, with Alison, with Kurt and with having to do rewrites in a schmotel of a hotel with no piano. Jack just sat there protected by a Lorne Greene look of concern. Then he just said, 'You have to tell me these things, Bobby. I'll get you a piano, I'll get you anything you want.' So last night . . . I'm at the stage door ready to go home and have a bath. Talking – or rather 'chalking' – with Simon having left me looking like the Phantom of the Opera.

He momentarily freezes.

Anyway . . . there was this kid. Kind of feisty looking – but not bad looking. And he turns round from the mail-rack and goes, 'Oi, you Bobby?' (*Pause.*) Like I'm the cat, right? I said, 'I'm Robert Buffet the musical director of this show.' You know? 'Can I help you?' I said. Well, it turned out he was some kid in the theatre, electrician or something, and Jack had hunted him out to provide me with . . . a piano. And he told me – his name's Tony – Tony or Tone – to come over the following night, so that I could have, his words, 'a tinkle on the Joanna'. A nation that pops weasels must inevitably, I suppose, tinkle Joannas. So, what the hell. If he's out to mug me, it's not like I've got any money. Is it, Jack?

Go to black.

Come up on a room in a London squat. It's dowdy but a youthful imagination has been at work on it. Bobby is lying on his back. Night.

You know Tony has never heard of Rodgers and Hammerstein. I happened to mention them the night I checked out of the Talisman. He just looked blank for a minute. Then he said, 'You got rogered in Hammersmith?' but he knew what I said all right. Even if he hadn't heard of them, and you know I wouldn't mind betting that he had. He just likes being smutty of course, like all Brits. Tony's got an excuse though because, you see, he has no discrimination. I mean just look at this place. Still it's better than where I was and it's not like we don't get on okay.

He looks around.

He's like me in a way. More than a touch of the Bohemian. And he can work his butt off. Comes in at all hours with eyes like a racoon. Just wish he didn't smell like one.

There is a pause.

Actually, I'm being a bit unfair because the other night he said he was going to clean up. Clean up or clear up, it was hard to tell, his diction's positively Brando. I was busy at 'the Joanna' trying to squeeze the tenor part into the tortuously cramped conditions of Kurt's talent. I'd just about decided to make him whistle the tune, when I heard Tony come back in making the kind of sticky noise like you can only make when you're in bare feet. Which he was. Then he sat down next to me and I could see he was in bare everything. I mean, totally, you know, bare. His skin was kind of olive like he'd been in the sun a long time ago and he'd got a crucifix on. You know, a little golden Jesus on one of those made to measure crosses. It was like he was Tarzan, swinging through the jungle of Tony's chest hair. He was just sitting there saying nothing and then he began to play the piano. I dunno . . . some cheesy little tune or other but like really badly with one finger. I just stared at the music paper, trying to make as many words as I could out of Boosey and Hawkes. I knew what was going down all right. As long as I didn't say anything you see, I could pretend that what was happening wasn't, oh, I don't know, the usual squalid thing. There'd been so much of that. But it struck me that if I didn't speak up we could both be there all night, so I said, 'Well, this is something of a surprise.' He said, 'Really? A surprise?' Then I said, 'No, frankly, I don't suppose it is. But I don't know what you're expecting.' 'Expecting?', he said. I said, 'Tony, we are not Hansel and Gretel. How much money do you want?' He looked really put out. He said, 'I don't want anything, Bob. Not from you. You're different.' 'Different?' I said. 'You mean you're doing this just for me?' 'Just for you,' he said. 'Well then,' I said, 'let's do it.' So we did. And there hasn't been anything like enough of that.

Go to black.

Come up on London squat. Bobby is looking at a kinetic sculpture of extremely dubious merit. It's more or less an abstract and appears to be of a woman.

I can't tell you how good that is. It's Alison to the life. Or whatever it is she uses as the next best thing. Tony said it only took him half an hour but he's just got to be joshing. You know he was actually going to give it to her as a first-night present. He's crazy. She can't sing, she can't act. What odds d'you want to give for her art appreciation. I told him to give it to someone . . . well, someone who knows art when he sees it. And he did.

Smell anything funny? Like burning flesh, for example. It's the reviews. We've already set one to music. The one that said my arrangements were like a whole suburb of gnomes being dropped in a blender and whipped into glop. We gave it a sort of Tony Bennett feel. We both wondered what glop was, but I didn't give a nostril full of rabbit shit because the guy was obviously disturbed. And, anyways, I don't care. Why should I care? I work in a store. I go home, the store gets burglarised. Don't cry for me, I'm the cleaner. That's all. And I mean the show is 'on'. Floating in formaldehyde maybe, but on. They can get some jerk from the Palladium to run round with the musical monkey wrench because on the first night Buffet here punched the clock. Punching Simon seemed like an even better idea but how can you floor a guy with only half a tongue. Especially when you find him face down in the lighting box crying his brains out. I sensed the first-night party had more or less peaked when Jack began the story of how he persuaded Gene Kelly to use rain instead of sleet. I heard Gene go 'I'm singing in the sleet' and I just knew I had to say something. Tony wanted to 'grab a bite' anyway, so we snooped around Soho till we found a little Italian cubby hole. It wasn't Soho like New York SoHo but I guess it had a sort of dinky charm. You know red and white check tablecloths, the usual cliché. Tony said it reminded him of that place in *The Godfather* where Al Pacino goes into the washroom and comes out with a gun. He asked what I'd do if he did that, you know, suddenly came back in and shot me. I said I'd be very sad and everything but that at least I wouldn't be left with the cheque. He said he was sorry that I was always the one who had to pay and I told him that I didn't mean that and anyway now he'd lost his job at the theatre there was no way he could. Besides, he pays me back in other ways. The best ways. I mean, I sat there in that little joint, answering his questions about the mafia and Kojak and God knows who else and I looked at the sparks the candlelight made in his eyes and I felt . . . I mean forget Harlequin romances and bullshit like that. This was . . . real. Here was this beautiful kid like something out of a Renaissance painting or whatever sitting in a restaurant talking to me because he wanted to. Before we go home to New York – yeah, 'we' – he wants to show me the Tate. He calls it the Tate and Lyle. I asked him why and he said, 'Because of the sugar.' The sugar? Maybe he's trying to say he's diabetic or something. I hope he isn't. Needles are a worry in New York right now. (*Pause.*) It's just as well he likes a kind of den feel to his surroundings: my place doesn't exactly have the smell of new paint, but then, of course, it just might if our young Raphael makes with the avocado green and eggshell magnolia. He's only coming on vacation. I don't know if he'll like it although he's already convinced he will. He's also convinced he's going to make a fortune. I gently reminded him that not everybody in New York cleans up. 'No, but I will,' he said.

Go to black.

We are in Bobby's Manhattan apartment. There are signs of efficient, fairly non-destructive burglary. Bobby is still in his coat from the journey. He holds a piece of paper in his hand.

'Dear Mr Music. We don't mess so that's why there isn't none. The buttermilk was off so we stuck it in the trash. Stuck cold tea in the Yucca 'cos the guy needed a serious drink. What are you doing with that recording of Mahler's fifth? It sucks to the sky. Check out the one with the L.A. Phil. Mahler needs sunshine and likewise your Yucca. Sincerely. The Nice guys.' (*Puts the message down.*) I guess they are nice. I mean, they've only taken what they wanted. Even if it happens to be everything with a plug on it. And all the records. Oh, I tell a lie. (*He bends down.*) I still have *The World of Anthony Newley*. Salvation. That means that while I'm popping my lid I can also pop my weasel. But that's a deliberate gesture. The sign of the true professional. The personal touch. (*He takes jacket off.*) Like the producer who provides not only the piano as requested, but a rent boy so professional he sees the client off at the airport. 'I said it wouldn't cost you, Bob. Jack's seen to everything.' Ever wanted people to level with you? Well, just get them in a departure lounge and watch them shoot from the hip. That's when Jack hit me with Alison and when Tony hit me with Jack. But Jack thinks he's done me a favour, though. Of course he does. He's been, you know, my ministering angel, beaming sunshine into Buffet's rainy little life. And who cares if it's only sunshine from a sunlamp so long as the cantankerous little faggot gets laid and stops giving us a hard time? I can't believe what you can say to someone once you've taken your clothes off.

He suddenly turns, breaks the record and any pots and vases to hand. The telephone rings. It rings a few times before Bobby can control himself sufficiently to answer it.

Hello . . . Hi, Jack . . . What? Who's been hijacked? No, I just said, 'Hi Jack.' I'm OK. Yeah, well I've been burglarised, no nothing's broken . . . (*Sits.*) Yeah, I've still got a bed. I sound weird. Yeah, well I think you've taken a liberty. I'm sure you meant well. What do you mean it was business? I see . . . he was my fee. Yes, it was better than money – oh, I'm glad it helps with your insurance. Good night, Jack.

He puts the telephone down and breaks down. Slowly he pulls himself together and walks to the door.

You know I need better security – more locks, a grill on the skylight. I mean no one's ever getting in here again. Not ever. I guess I'll check out Joe Allen's, get my eye teeth into a nice chunk of gossip. It's all very straight down there. And when you know where you stand, you can stand forever.

He goes out. The camera stays on the room for a moment before fading to black.